AF255213

Whatever Happened to Christianity?

Whatever Happened to Christianity?

A *Tafsir* for Muslim Scholars and Thinkers

FRED FARROKH

WIPF *&* STOCK · Eugene, Oregon

WHATEVER HAPPENED TO CHRISTIANITY?
A *Tafsir* for Muslim Scholars and Thinkers

Wipf & Stock
An Imprint of Wipf and Stock Publishers
199 W. 8th Ave., Suite 3
Eugene, OR 97401

www.wipfandstock.com

PAPERBACK ISBN: 978-1-6667-7182-4
HARDCOVER ISBN: 978-1-6667-7183-1
EBOOK ISBN: 978-1-6667-7184-8

05/18/23

To Muslim scholars and thinkers throughout the world

Contents

PART III: AN INQUIRY INTO THE RELIABILITY OF THE PORTRAYAL OF THE LORD JESUS' LIFE AND TEACHING AS REPRESENTED IN THE NEW TESTAMENT

PART IV: OUTSTANDING CHALLENGES

Preface:
Searching for *as-Sirat al-Mustaqeem*

Like many Muslim boys and girls, I learned early in life to pray to Allah for guidance toward the straight path, or *as-Sirat al-Mustaqeem:*[1] *Ihdina as-Sirat al-Mustaqeem, as-Sirat al-ladhina anamta alaihim, ghairil maghdubi alaihim wa la Daalleen. Amin.* "Guide us along the Straight Path, the Path of those you have blessed—not the path You are displeased with, or those who are astray. Amen" (al-Fatiha, ayat 6 and 7).[2] And the last phrase, *wa la Daalleen, Amin,* was always drawn out for emphasis. The Arabic reads as follows:

أَهْدِنَا ٱلصِّرَٰطَ ٱلْمُسْتَقِيمَ
صِرَٰطَ ٱلَّذِينَ أَنْعَمْتَ عَلَيْهِمْ غَيْرِ ٱلْمَغْضُوبِ عَلَيْهِمْ وَلَا ٱلضَّآلِّينَ

Over half a century has passed from the days of my childhood until now. During that time, I have become a follower of the Lord Jesus Christ. As I write to my Muslim friends, I want you to know I am a Christian.

---

1. Arabic nouns include case endings depending upon the role the noun plays in a sentence. This affects the spelling in transliteration of *as-Sirat al-Mustaqeem.* Since changing spellings based on grammatical case may only produce confusion in a book not written in Arabic, I have chosen to utilize a uniform transliteration of *as-Sirat al-Mustaqeem* (that is, objective case) for "the Straight Path." Also, for simplicity, I have not used underlying dots for Arabic guttural consonants.

2. All qur'anic quotations in English are from https://quran.com/.

Indeed, in this life, we search for that straight path. The Lord Jesus gave similar instructions to His disciples: "Enter through the narrow gate; for the gate is wide and the way is broad that leads to destruction, and there are many who enter through it. For the gate is small and the way is narrow that leads to life, and there are few who find it" (Matt 7:13–14).[3]

The believer in this lifetime is beset by one great limitation. Those who have died do not return to this life to report the truths they may learn in the afterlife. The deceased alcoholic cannot return to this life to warn his alcoholic friends, "Do not drink." The atheist who has died does not return to this life to tell his friends that he has discovered there is a God. Neither can he warn them of the awaiting Day of Judgment, the *Yom ad-Din*, and that every person will stand before God on that day. Neither Muslims nor Christians return to this world after their deaths to report who has gone to heaven and who has gone to hell.

Jesus advised us that there may be some surprises in eternity. He told a parable known as "The Rich Man and Lazarus" in which a rich man died and found himself in torment. The rich man observed another deceased soul, Lazarus, dwelling across a chasm in comfort with Abraham, the father of believers. The rich man begged Abraham, "I beg you, father, send Lazarus to my family, for I have five brothers. Let him warn them, so that they will not also come to this place of torment" (Luke 16:27–28). Abraham indicates it is not possible for the dead to return to warn the living. Yet, Abraham states that those who live on the earth have Moses and the prophets to guide them.

Those among the living must therefore rely on the wisdom of others, such as the learned, the prophets, and holy writings. Humans need guidance. Muslims have asked the Almighty to reveal that guidance.

People must also look deep within themselves to find the courage to face the most important question of this life: Where is *as-Sirat al-Mustaqeem*? Many do not have the courage to face

3. The New American Standard Bible (1995) is used for quotations of Scripture throughout.

this question. However, people cannot defer this decision to others. Though it may be a slow process, all people are responsible to search for *as-Sirat al-Mustaqeem*.

As Muslim children, we may have recited these words many times without thinking about their importance. Muslim adults will recite them in each of the seventeen *rakat* per day during prayers. Now is the time to think about what we have been praying. In this short book, we will take a deep look into our quest for *as-Sirat al-Mustaqeem*.

I have dedicated this book to Muslim scholars and thinkers. Muslims and Christians alike understand that all theological questions are important. After all, theology is the study of God. It also becomes clear that some theological issues rise above others in prominence. Some urgent questions emerge as existential to a belief system.

As a person who was born and raised Muslim, but who is now a Christian, I have been pondering for some time the theological question considered in this book. Perhaps my thought process has been stimulated while teaching a church history class several times in the Muslim-majority country of Albania.

I believe this question at hand—whatever happened to Christianity?—is existential to the innate viability of Islam. If Jesus Christ presented himself as a mortal messenger of *tawhid*, how could a movement of over two billion people arise who consider Him a Lord, a God, and a Savior?

My contribution to this conversation does not resolve the dilemma at hand. Therefore, I encourage open-minded Muslims to read along and think along. Christians and others may be interested in the discussion also; we live in a time of interfaith dialog. After all, we are all on a journey which the Almighty has allowed us to walk together in our days upon this earth.

Rev. Dr. Fred Farrokh
Tirana, Albania,
1 March 2023 / 9th Shaban 1444
www.whateverhappenedtochristianity.com

Acknowledgments

I thank Matthew Bennett, Joshua Fletcher, Steve Krstulovich, Don McCurry, and Duane Miller for reviewing the manuscript and provided helpful edits and commentary. I thank Adam Simnowitz for sharing with me his notes and research on the Holy Trinity.

I thank my instructors at Elim Bible Institute and College, as well as Assemblies of God Theological Seminary, for their spiritual and biblical impartation in my life. I also acknowledge those who have pastored me in the faith. Each demonstrated a commitment to and love for the Bible. Countless other people have imparted spiritual blessings in my life.

I would like to thank God for the memory of a personal mentor, the late Rev. Dick Dreyer, who served Christ in the Middle East. He frequently stated that he prayed for me and my family every day. He passed on to his eternal reward the year prior to the publication of this book.

I also thank my parents, Dr. Alinaghi and Edna Farrokh, who always modeled hard work and faith in God. I hope I will be able to also model these same characteristics for my own children.

I thank the team at Wipf and Stock for their ready assistance throughout the publishing process. I naturally stand responsible for all shortcomings of this publication.

PART I

The Islamic Claim of Christians Having Gone Astray

Chapter 1

The Necessity of Christians Going Astray in the Islamic Narrative

I understand that a wide range of readers may open this book, including Muslims, Christians, and others. All are welcome to incorporate this book into their spiritual journey. Immediately below, I have written about things and ideas that will be well known to many Muslims. Yet I include it for readers who may lack that familiarity.

The first sura, al-Fatiha, literally "opens" the Qur'an. This sura is also a prayer which Muslims pray every day. That prayer includes a request for guidance into the Straight Path, *as-Sirat al-Mustaqeem*. That path is the *sirat* of those upon whom the Almighty has shown favor. Muslims earnestly pray not to tread upon the path of those who have gone astray.

The Qur'an does not specifically mention within al-Fatiha who has gone astray. Abi bin Hatim asked the Prophet of Islam for clarification in a hadith that is considered *sahih* (authentic) and is quoted by at-Tirmidhi and Abu Dawud:

> Narrated Adi bin Hatim: I asked Allah's Messenger about the Statement of Allah: "*Gharil maghdubi ʿalaihim* [not (the way) of those who earned Your Anger]," he replied:

"They are the Jews." And 2: "*Walad dallin* (nor of those who went astray)," he replied: "The Christians, and they are the ones who went astray."[1]

The theological urgency of the question under study prevails regardless of any interpretation of Q1:7, in which Christians, *an-Nasara*, are not specifically named. The straying of Christians emerges as an overarching metanarrative issue. The viability of Islam requires it.

Nevertheless, the interpretation that Christians have gone astray is well known by Muslims. *Tafsir al-Jalalayn* records that it is Christians who have strayed. Ibn Kathir, in his *Great Commentary on the Qur'an*, gives the following tafsir for Q1:7:

> Allah asserted that the two paths He described here are both misguided when He repeated the negation "not." These two paths are the paths of the Christians and Jews, a fact that the believer should beware of so that he avoids them. The path of the believers is knowledge of the truth and abiding by it. In comparison, the Jews abandoned practicing the religion, while the Christians lost the true knowledge. This is why anger descended upon the Jews, while being described as "led astray" is more appropriate of the Christians.[2]

THE IMPORTANCE OF CHRISTIANS HAVING GONE ASTRAY TO THE ISLAMIC NARRATIVE

In Islam, Jesus is a mortal prophet who is the messenger of *tawhid*. *Tawhid* forms the central tenet of Islam, stating that Allah is indivisibly One God without plurality in his Unity. In the preface to the English translation of Muhammad Abduh's classic work *Risalat at-Tauhid* (*Theology of Unity*) (1895), translators Ishaq Musa'ad and Kenneth Cragg are instructive:

1. Hilali and Khan, *Interpretation*, 15–16.
2. Ibn Kathir, "Commentaries for 1.7," para. 9.

It must be remembered that *Tauhid* is a causative and intensive noun and never means "unity," still less "unitariness," as an abstract state. It is aggressive, so to speak, antiseptic: it means intolerant of all pluralism, in the ardent subjugation of all that flouts or doubts it.[3]

In Islam, all messengers served the same purpose to warn their respective generations. The Qur'an states that there is no distinction between the various messengers, among whom Jesus is one:

> The Messenger firmly believes in what has been revealed to him from his Lord, and so do the believers. They all believe in Allah, His angels, His Books, and His messengers. They proclaim, "*We make no distinction between any of His messengers.*" And they say, "We hear and obey. 'We seek' Your forgiveness, our Lord! And to You alone is the final return.[4]

All Islamic prophets had the same essential message: worship Allah, the One; do not worship idols; and prepare for *Yom ad-Din*. The Islamic Jesus promotes this narrative in verses such as Q5:72:

> Those who say, "Allah is the Messiah, son of Mary," have certainly fallen into disbelief. The Messiah himself said, "O Children of Israel! Worship Allah—my Lord and your Lord." Whoever associates others with Allah in worship will surely be forbidden Paradise by Allah. Their home will be the Fire. And the wrongdoers will have no helpers.

A similar statement is made by Jesus in the same sura, al-Ma'idah, Q5:116:

> And on Judgment Day Allah will say, "O Jesus, son of Mary! Did you ever ask the people to worship you and your mother as gods besides Allah?" He will answer,

3. Musa'ad and Cragg. "Introduction," 12.

4. Sura Baqara 2:285, emphasis added. In some cases, I have removed diacritical carrot marks placed in the translated text to indicate words supplied for readability. While helpful in such a translation, those same marks may impede readability in book form. Any reader may consult the multiple available English translations of the Qur'an, or the Arabic, for cross-checking.

> "Glory be to You! How could I ever say what I had no
> right to say? If I had said such a thing, you would have
> certainly known it. You know what is hidden within me,
> but I do not know what is within You. Indeed, You alone
> are the Knower of all unseen."

These verses support the Islamic doctrine that Jesus is a mortal messenger of *tawhid*. This fits within the standard Islamic narrative regarding the continuity of the prophetic ministry throughout time.

Muslims who have studied the Bible or Christian theology understand that Christians have a far different belief about Jesus than is presented by the standard Islamic narrative. Christians believe that Jesus is the divine Savior who came from heaven to earth to die on the cross for sinful people. Thereafter, He rose from the dead and ascended into heaven.[5]

Perhaps nothing could be further from the standard Islamic narrative. Islamic scholar and author Tarif Khalidi notes this marked chasm:

> Clearly there is *something* about Jesus which makes his
> qur'anic image so utterly different from the Jesus of the
> Gospels. . . . He is the only prophet in the Qur'an who is
> deliberately made to distance himself from the doctrines
> that his community is said to hold about him.[6]

Khalidi correctly notes that the qur'anic picture of Jesus is "utterly different" from the biblical picture of Jesus. Muslims explain this difference by contending that Christians have gone astray. For that reason, a further study of the qur'anic concept of going astray now follows.

---

5. Many English Bibles capitalize pronouns which refer to deity. This includes the New American Standard Bible (1995) which is quoted in this book. Christians often follow this practice in general writing of prose. This may create some confusion regarding capitalization since the Islamic Jesus is not divine, but the biblical Jesus is divine. To mitigate confusion, this book will utilize this Christian tradition of capitalizing pronouns in which the referent is divine. Readers are encouraged to pay close attention to the context in which pronouns are used.

6. Khalidi, *Muslim Jesus*, 11—12, emphasis in original.

GOING ASTRAY

Christians have been identified in the interpretation of Sura Fatiha as *ad-Daalleen*, "those who have gone astray." The Arabic root *daad—lam—lam* occurs 191 times in the Qur'an.[7] It appears in various forms as a noun, verb, or participle.

Various passages of the Qur'an condemn Christians for having gone astray. Sura 4:116 announces that those who commit *shirk*—associating partners with Allah—have committed the unpardonable sin and have gone astray: "Surely Allah does not forgive associating others with Him in worship, but forgives anything else of whoever He wills. Indeed, whoever associates others with Allah has clearly gone far astray."

This verse describes the person who has gone far astray. Here the root *daad, lam, lam* is used in consecutive words in two different forms. The second half of the verse includes a triple condemnation, *dalla dalaalan ba'eedan*. The one committing *shirk* has 1. lost the way, 2. straying, 3. far away. Paradise closes its doors to such a misguided one; he has committed the unpardonable sin.

Sura Nisa' includes several other condemnatory uses of "going astray." Q4:44 features a double usage of this word: "Have you ⸢O Prophet⸣ not seen those who were given a portion of the Scriptures *yet trade it for misguidance* and wish to see *you deviate from the Right Path?*"[8] According to this verse, these misguided ones even sought to lead the Prophet astray.

Verse 46 of Sura Nisa' provides the context as a rebuke of the Jews. But it is soon followed by verse 48 in reference to those who commit *shirk*, the Christians: "Indeed, Allah does not forgive associating others with Him in worship, but forgives anything else of whoever He wills. And whoever associates others with Allah has indeed committed a grave sin."

Moving beyond the fourth sura, the sixteenth sura, an-Nahl, renders a usage of *daad, lam, lam* which reiterates that all prophets delivered a similar message, though some of the disbelievers have

7. qur'anic Arabic Corpus, "Dll."
8. Emphasis added.

gone astray: "We surely sent a messenger to every community, saying, 'Worship Allah and shun false gods.' But some of them were guided by Allah, *while others were destined to stray.* So travel throughout the land and see the fate of the deniers!" (Q16:36).[9] This brief qur'anic word study of the word associated with "straying" indicates that Christians are *ad-Daalleen*, "those who have gone astray."

THE URGENCY OF THE QUESTION

Several experiences dissipate the urgency of the question for Muslims regarding when, where, and how Christians may have gone astray. Many Muslims are kindhearted and empathetic people. One may hear these Muslims positively affirm that Christians have a prophet—Jesus—and a holy book—*al-Injil*. Though these same Muslims feel that the faith of Christians remains incomplete, they may likewise feel that the faith of Christians is the most complete of any non-Muslim community. For them, Christians may be "one step away" from the complete truth which Islam provides. But at least they are on the path of monotheistic belief.

A second observation is that in some Islamic nations Christians only comprise a small minority. This may give subconscious reassurance to Muslims that Christians do not enjoy God's favor. After all, there is strength in numbers. Muslims may assume that such disfavor may be the result of the Christians having gone astray.

In other contexts, many Christians maintain only a nominal Christianity. Perhaps they attend church only twice a year on the major holidays of Christmas (Christ's Birth) and Easter (Christ's Resurrection). Muslims who observe this may likewise conclude that Christians have gone astray due to a perceived lack of commitment.

In other cases, Muslims may not live in proximity to any Christians. These Muslims may not think about Christians at all. Or they may merely rely on reports about Christians from external

9. Emphasis added. It is beyond the scope of this inquiry to determine whether people used their active will to go astray or whether they were destined by the Almighty to stray.

news sources. These realities may cloud the issue and diffuse the urgency of the question which all Muslims must answer: If Christians went astray, when, where and how did they go astray?

This question is not only important to the Islamic narrative; it emerges as a necessity. Christians believe that Jesus is the divine Savior who came from heaven to die on the cross for sinful people. The core Christian beliefs will be analyzed fully in chapters 6–9. On the other hand, Islam teaches that Jesus is merely a mortal messenger of *tawhid*. In Christianity, Jesus is divine. In Islam, he cannot be divine. He must be a mortal messenger. Therefore, both messages cannot simultaneously be true. At least one must be false. Islam contends that Christians have gone astray in elevating Jesus beyond the status of a mortal messenger.

CONCLUSION

"Going astray" comprises a recurring theological theme in the Qur'an. Christians have committed an unpardonable sin of *shirk* by attributing divinity to Jesus. Thus, they comprise a class of people who have gone astray. They are condemned by the Qur'an. Praying Muslims, according to al-Fatiha, seek to avoid following in their footsteps.

But when, where, and how did Christians go astray? Muslim scholars and thinkers will want to know the answer to this question. To this question, the inquiry now turns.

Chapter 2

An Inquiry into When, Where, and How the Christians May Have Gone Astray

As the previous chapter described, a marked difference exists between the standard Islamic narrative and the biblical narrative regarding Jesus Christ. Islam teaches that Jesus is a mortal prophet in the line of other prophets. The Bible, on the other hand, describes Jesus as Lord, God, and Savior, whose mission was to come to the earth and die on the cross to pay for the sins of humanity, thus restoring them to a personal relationship with God.

The Bible teaches that when Jesus died on the cross, He declared "It is finished" (John 19:30). That is, God's plan of salvation was finished. The biblical narrative presents no need for a "final prophet," known as *khatam an-nabiyeen* (Q33:40). Therefore, Jesus' qur'anic statement rings as non-sequitur in Q61:6: "And remember when Jesus, son of Mary, said, 'O children of Israel! I am truly Allah's messenger to you, confirming the Torah which came before me, and giving good news of a messenger after me whose name will be Ahmad.'" This verse epitomizes Jesus' two main roles in the Islamic theological structure: first, to declare he was simply a messenger, and second, to prophesy about another prophet coming after him, specifically, Ahmad, that is, Muhammad.

The Islamic narrative flows from the Qur'an and Hadith literature. If this narrative is untrue, then the whole credibility of Islam collapses. If the biblical narrative, which is believed by Christians, is true, then there is no need for a forthcoming final prophet, *al-khatam*, or any final religion after the birth of Christianity, such as Islam. For these reasons, the investigation into when, where, and how the Christians may have gone astray becomes extremely important for Muslims and the credibility of Islam. This investigation will probe these areas.

WHEN, WHERE, AND HOW MIGHT CHRISTIANITY HAVE GONE ASTRAY

To set a timeline with which most readers will already be familiar, the prophet of Islam was born six centuries after Jesus the son of Mary. In one of His last commands to His apostles, Jesus called them together in Galilee and commissioned them to go into all the world and make disciples of all nations:

> All authority has been given to Me in heaven and on earth. 19 Go therefore and make disciples of all the nations, baptizing them in the name of the Father and the Son and the Holy Spirit, 20 teaching them to observe all that I commanded you; and lo, I am with you always, even to the end of the age. (Matt 28:18–20)

Beginning first in Jerusalem, these twelve apostles indeed traveled very far to spread the gospel. Thomas is reported to have gone furthest. This apostle, sometimes called Doubting Thomas, traveled all the way to India, preaching his way across that great distance. In India, Thomas planted the church and was martyred in Chennai (Madras) about AD 72. This occurred approximately forty years after Jesus' commissioning mentioned above.

Peter, according to church historical traditions, preached in Antioch, Corinth, Asia Minor (modern-day Turkey), and Rome.

His brother, the apostle Andrew, preached in Georgia, Romania, Cyprus, and possibly Scotland. The apostle John, of whom we will hear later, preached at Ephesus. The apostle Bartholomew, also known as Nathaniel, preached in Armenia and Mesopotamia. Thaddeus also preached in Armenia. This comprises just a partial list of where Jesus' twelve apostles preached.

Jesus' disciples included not only these twelve, but many others also. The Gospels describe an inner core of three disciples—Peter, James, and John—within the twelve. Jesus also had a wider circle of seventy which he sent on short-term missions according to Luke's Gospel, chapter 10. Both men and women followed Jesus and the apostolic band. Some of these women provided for Jesus out of their own resources (Luke 8:1–3). Jesus appeared multiple times to His disciples after His resurrection. Paul states that the resurrected Christ also appeared to more than 500 people at the same time (1 Cor 15:6).

Immediately after Jesus' ascension to heaven, Luke describes in Acts 1:15 that 120 followers of Jesus were praying together in an upper room in Jerusalem. Within ten days, 3,000 people repented and believed in Christ on the Day of Pentecost (Acts 2:41). These Pentecost celebrants came from Persia, Egypt, North Africa, Arab lands, and other places, according to the second chapter of Acts. Though not all of them would have become preachers, two conclusions spring from this narrative. First, the movement of Jesus, which would soon become called *Christians*, grew very quickly. Second, it dispersed rapidly into a large geographic area.

If the Christians had gone astray, therefore, it must have occurred very early. Had these disciples erred very early after the ascension of Jesus, then they could have sown a uniformly errant and deceptive message around the world. That scenario would require that Jesus presented himself as a mortal messenger of *tawhid*, but that his disciples somehow elevated him to divine status and then preached that message around the world. This would have required a conspiracy. Yet it is often said that few people will voluntarily die for a lie that they have fabricated; all of the twelve apostles, except for John and the traitor Judas Iscariot, are recorded as having been martyred for Jesus' sake.

Any argument that the main body of Christians went astray long after the birth of the Christian movement, but before the advent of Islam, seems implausible. If a teacher, or a subset of Christians, had gone astray decades or centuries after the advent of Christianity, then the other groups would have retained the original message—ostensibly one that featured Jesus as the mortal messenger of *tawhid*. The guardians of the original, orthodox[1] message would then have identified the threatening error to protect the movement and its adherents from it.

Indeed, all movements—political, social, and religious—face the challenge of heretical threats, as well as fragmentation. Orthodox Islam has faced and combatted these challenges over fourteen centuries. Orthodox Christianity has faced similar threats and heresies. However, the orthodox Christian mainstream has always maintained that Jesus is the Lord and divine Savior. It has condemned heretical movements, such as Arianism, which will be described below.

Since the apostles of Jesus preached the same basic biblical narrative about Jesus as Lord, then any deception or straying which might have occurred among them must have occurred right at the beginning of the Christian era. And this must have occurred while all the apostles were still together in Judea or Galilee. Indeed, they must have gone astray for the standard Islamic narrative to be true.

One reason Muslims may tend not to dwell on the specifics of Christians going astray comes from confounding the cause and effect of the problem. According to standard Islamic thinking, the Jews sinned by rejecting Jesus, even though they accepted all prophets up until Moses. Christians, similarly, went astray by accepting all prophets up until Jesus. But then they failed to accept Muhammad as a prophet. Muslims believe that they themselves

---

1. There is a distinction between "Orthodox" as one branch of Christianity (ie, Catholic, Protestant, and Orthodox) and "orthodox" meaning the mainstream, non-heretical teaching of the historic body of Christ. The former is capitalized; the latter is lower-case, unless beginning a sentence.

accept all prophets and all holy books up until Muhammad and the Qur'an. Many Muslims will think it to be an easy answer: "Christians have gone astray because they did not believe in Muhammad."

However, Christian rejection of Muhammad only happened six centuries after the time of Christ. This must be considered the effect. The cause must be the previous adoption of some belief system that rejected the teachings of Muhammad that Christ was a mortal messenger of *tawhid*. Where, when, and how did Christians develop that belief that Christ was not merely a messenger of *tawhid*, but Lord, God, and Savior?

ISLAMIC EXPLANATIONS REGARDING CHRISTIANS STRAYING

Three leading Islamic theories have emerged as to when, where, and how Christians have gone astray. The first attends the circumstances of Jesus' alleged crucifixion. The second indicts the apostle Paul as the one who led Christians astray. The third comprises the Islamic doctrine of *tahrif*, or corruption of Scripture. Each will be considered below.

The Appearance of the Crucifixion

The Qur'an provides the following explanation regarding the crucifixion of Jesus. The Jews are condemned in Q4:156–58:

> For their denial and outrageous accusation against Mary, and for boasting, "We killed the Messiah, Jesus, son of Mary, the messenger of Allah." But they neither killed nor crucified him—it was only made to appear so. Even those who argue for this crucifixion are in doubt. They have no knowledge whatsoever—only making assumptions. They certainly did not kill him, Rather, Allah raised him up to Himself. And Allah is Almighty, All-Wise.

In this passage, "it was only made to appear" (*shubbiha lahum*) that Jesus had been crucified. The Qur'an does not explicitly state that a substitute was provided. Neither does the text state whom that substitute might have been.

The majority Islamic view holds that a substitute was crucified instead of Jesus. Various substitute candidates have been advanced, such as Judas Iscariot and Simon of Cyrene. Ibn Kathir writes:

> Ibn Abbas said, "Just before Allah raised Jesus to the Heavens, Jesus went to his disciples, who were twelve inside the house. When he arrived, his hair was dripping with water (as if he had just had a bath) and he said, 'There are those among you who will disbelieve in me twelve times after you had believed in me.' He then asked, 'Who among you will volunteer for his appearance to be transformed into mine, and be killed in my place? Whoever volunteers for that, he will be with me in Paradise.' One of the youngest ones among them volunteered, but Jesus asked him to sit down. Jesus asked again for a volunteer, and the same young man volunteered and Jesus asked him to sit down again. Then the young man volunteered a third time and Jesus said, 'You will be that man,' and the resemblance of Jesus was cast over that man while Jesus ascended to Heaven from a hole in the roof of the house. When the Jews came looking for Jesus, they found that young man and crucified him."[2]

Muslims have long debated the plausibility and the ethics of such a substitution. Modern scholar Mahmoud Ayoub cites Fakr al-Din al-Razi (d. 1209) as addressing the problems associated with substitutionism—the likeness of one projected onto another. First, "no social norm such as marriage or property rights could be ascertained."[3] Second, it would ruin the idea of historical testimony.

For the purposes of this inquiry, Ibn Kathir's substitution theory provides only an explanation of how Christians may have

2. Ibn Kathir, "Commentary on Sura 4," para. 33

3. Razi, in Ayoub, *Muslim View*, 164.

been misled or gone astray in relation to the crucifixion.[4] It would not explain how Christians went astray from Islamic beliefs by upholding anti-qur'anic doctrines such as the Trinity—that God is eternally existent as Father, Son, and Holy Spirit. This departure from Islamic *tawhid* is perhaps the greatest difference between qur'anic and biblical beliefs, so any explanation of Christian straying must account for it.

Paul and the Hijacking of Christianity

A common explanation presented by Muslims over the centuries for the straying of Christians places the blame at the feet of the apostle Paul. Bilal Muhammad writes: "The late Muslim polemicist Ahmed Deedat described Paul as 'the real founder of Christianity' and the cause of division between Christian and Islamic theology."[5] Paul's biography will be explored in the next chapter. His relationship to the other apostles will be considered in chapter 5. Muslims may reason that since Paul was not one of the original twelve, he could have wrested control of the movement from the original apostles—those who would have been taught by Jesus that he himself was a mortal messenger of *tawhid*. Paul, then, could have deceived and misled Christians by teaching them doctrines such as the Holy Trinity, the divinity of Jesus, salvation by faith in Christ, and the centrality of blood sacrifices to forgiveness of sins.

Due to the prominence of the contention that Paul misguided Christians, chapter 5 will focus on that possibility. Additional material will set Paul's contribution to Christianity in its context.

The Islamic Contention of Tahrif

Christians and Muslims have engaged each other for many centuries regarding the Islamic allegation of *tahrif*—the distortion or

4. On the other hand, such a theory provides Jesus with some type of superhuman ending. He does not die but lives on and will return to earth.

5. Muhammad, "Muslim Perspectives," para. 1.

corruption of Scripture on the part of Jews and Christians. Many books and treatises have been written on this subject. As such, a full treatment of *tahrif* exceeds the scope of this short book. However, since *tahrif* does impact directly on the inquiry of Christians straying, it must be considered by Christians as well as Muslim scholars and thinkers.

Though the noun *tahrif* does not appear in the Qur'an, the Arabic verb based on its roots, *H-r-f*, occurs four times in the Qur'an: Q2:75; 4:46; 5:13; and 5:41.[6] Sura Baqara, the longest sura, includes a historical progression from Adam onward. It recounts the favors of Allah upon the Jewish people. Yet, they are accused of corrupting the word of Allah in Q2:75: "Do you believers still expect them to be true to you, though a group of them would hear the word of Allah then knowingly corrupt it after understanding it?" Though this rebuke addresses Jews not Christians, the underlying question comes forth from the term "a group of them," *fariiquun minhum*. If a subset of the whole group is guilty of distortion or corruption of Scripture, may there not still be a faithful core group who have preserved both the text and a faithful interpretation thereof?

Muslims and Christians have furthermore long discussed whether the doctrine of *tahrif* pertains to the corruption of the text itself, or simply a corruption of interpretation. Christians readily concede that pseudo-Christian heretics have corrupted the interpretation of the Bible. Often this stems from illogical or out-of-context interpretations of Scripture. Christians, like Muslims, retain principles of interpretation known as *hermeneutics*. These principles have been used to detect and correct heresy.

Regarding any allegation of corruption of the actual biblical text, Martin Accad explored the original Arabic commentaries of the *mufassiruun* (commentators) on this topic. He concludes that the stronger, condemnatory position of actual textual corruption only emerged with Ibn Hazm in the eleventh century in Spain. Prior to that, Accad argues, Muslim commentators expressed less concern over textual corruption of the Bible.[7]

6. qur'anic Arabic Corpus, "Hrf."

7. See Accad, *Sacred Misinterpretation,* especially chapter 6, "Muslim

Indeed, the section in Sura Baqara quoted above, begins as follows in Q2:40–41:

> O children of Israel! Remember My favors upon you. Fulfil your covenant and I will fulfil Mine, and stand in awe of Me alone. Believe in My revelations which confirm your Scriptures. Do not be the first to deny them or trade them for a fleeting gain. And be mindful of Me.

While various qur'anic verses such as 2:41 indicate Jews and Christians held a reliable Bible in their hands at the advent of Islam, the New Testament constitutes a problem for the standard Islamic narrative. If Christians have a bona fide Scripture from God that teaches Jesus is the divine Savior, then what to make of the Qur'an which denies this teaching? As stated above, for Islam to be true—and even for Islam to be necessary—Christians *must* have gone astray.

The *tahrif* question can be applied to this inquiry as follows: If Muslims are asked when, where, and how Christians have gone astray, they may respond by saying, "By corrupting their Scriptures." The follow-up question naturally would be: "Then, when, where, and how were their Scriptures corrupted?"

In pursuance of this question, chapter 4 will investigate the transmission of Jesus' life and teaching into the New Testament record. Prior to that, chapter 3 will examine the relationship of the Lord Jesus Christ to the eight writers of the New Testament, from which Christian beliefs are derived.

Strategies in Approaching the Bible."

PART II

Bridges within the Early Church

Chapter 3

The Relationship of the Lord Jesus to the Great Eight Witnesses

THE INQUIRY INTO WHETHER Christians have gone astray requires an understanding of what Christians believe and how those beliefs developed. Similarities exist in how Christian and Muslim beliefs came to be. Yet, enough differences exist that Muslim scholars and thinkers will need to possess a deep understanding of these differences to conduct an accurate evaluation.

THE HOLY BIBLE

The beliefs of Christians derive from the Holy Bible. The Bible is divided into two main parts—the Old Testament and the New Testament. The Old Testament contains thirty-nine books written over 1,000 years by approximately thirty writing authors who can be likened to writing prophets. These thirty-nine books include the five books of Moses, known as the Torah or Pentateuch, as well as the Psaltery, known as the book of Psalms, many of which were written by David. Other significant Old Testament writers include Joshua, Solomon, Isaiah, Jeremiah, and Daniel.

Malachi's short book of prophecy constitutes the final book in the Old Testament chronology. Thereafter followed 400 "Silent Years" until the birth of John the Baptist, known to Muslims as Yahya. Then, a few months later, Jesus Christ was born in Bethlehem.[1]

When Jesus came to His own Jewish people, some received Him, while others rejected Him. This created a split within Judaism which exists to this day. Those who embraced Jesus and believed in Him catalyzed what can be considered "Messianic Judaism." As that movement spread among the non-Jewish gentiles, it grew, evolved, and contextualized into what we now call "Christianity," with its various branches and denominations. The overwhelming majority of Christians today are gentiles. Those Jewish adherents who rejected Jesus developed a theological trajectory which is known as "Rabbinic Judaism," which also has many branches and denominations.[2]

COMPARING CHRISTIAN AND ISLAMIC VIEWS OF WRITTEN REVELATION

Islam and Christianity are similar in that the central figure in each religion did not leave a written revelation. The prophet of Islam, according to Uthmanic Recension, is believed to have preached his messages over twenty-three years to believers who memorized them. Later, the caliph Uthman ordered these messages be written

1. A series of writings emerged during the so-called 400 "Silent Years" which are not accepted as parts of the Bible by Jewish believers or by most Christian believers. However, some Christians later accepted some of these books, known as the Apocrypha. Since these writings occur in the "Intertestamental Period," they do not present beliefs about Jesus Christ. Although Jesus quoted many Old Testament verses and books, He never quoted any verse from the Apocrypha. Thus, He did not give scriptural authority to those writings. And since the qur'anic accusation of Christians going astray largely centers on them committing *shirk* regarding Jesus, the Intertestamental Period does not constitute a central point in this inquiry.

2. Islam, like Judaism, Christianity, and other religions, features a set of core beliefs, as well as various branches and denominations. All human associations, whether political, religious, or cultural, tend to split, fragment, and denominationalize over time. Fragmentation itself does not determine whether the core message of a religion or movement is true or false.

down in a form known as "al-Qur'an," literally, "The Recitations." Al-Bukhari records this process as follows:

> Narrated Anas bin Malik: Hudhaifa bin Al-Yaman came to Uthman at the time when the people of Sham and the people of Iraq were Waging war to conquer Arminya and Adharbijan: Hudhaifa was afraid of their (the people of Sham and Iraq) differences in the recitation of the Qur'an, so he said to Uthman, "O chief of the Believers! Save this nation before they differ about the Book (Qur'an) as Jews and the Christians did before."
>
> So Uthman sent a message to Hafsa saying, "Send us the manuscripts of the Qur'an so that we may compile the qur'anic materials in perfect copies and return the manuscripts to you." Hafsa sent it to Uthman. Uthman then ordered Zaid bin Thabit, Abdullah bin Az-Zubair, Sa'id bin Al-As and Abdur-Rahman bin Harith bin Hisham to rewrite the manuscripts in perfect copies. Uthman said to the three Quraishi men, "In case you disagree with Zaid bin Thabit on any point in the Qur'an, then write it in the dialect of Quraish, [since] the Qur'an was revealed in their tongue." They did so, and when they had written many copies, Uthman returned the original manuscripts to Hafsa. Uthman sent to every Muslim province one copy of what they had copied, and ordered that all the other qur'anic materials, whether written in fragmentary manuscripts or whole copies, be burnt.[3]

Neither did Jesus write down what He wanted His followers to believe. Instead, He taught a group of disciples intensively over three years. The core group of twelve disciples became known as the twelve apostles whom Jesus commissioned to go into all the world and preach the good news about Himself. Three of the Twelve would go on to write books that are part of the New Testament, which codifies what Christians believe. The Twelve were an important part of Jesus' movement, but a much wider circle of people heard Him speak and teach, including seventy, as mentioned above, whom He even commissioned for short-term apostolic ministry.

3. Bukhari, "Virtues."

In assessing when, where, and how Christians may have gone astray, it is necessary to study what Christians believe. Those beliefs come from the Bible. The life of Jesus is featured in the New Testament. The New Testament represents the apostles' teaching, which they learned from Jesus. While the Old Testament was written in Hebrew, the New Testament was written in Greek. The Old Testament contains thirty-nine books, while the New Testament contains twenty-seven books. Muslim scholars and thinkers may think of the Holy Bible, therefore, as something more of a holy library. Nevertheless, the books are interrelated and have a central message focusing on the Lord Jesus Christ.

Islam teaches that the Qur'an preexisted "on eternal tablets," *fi lawhin mahfuuzin*, according to Q85:22. The content of these tablets would therefore have come down to this world via *tanzeel* (descent) in installments over twenty-three years. This process could be compared technologically to "direct download" of the data to the recipient.

INTRODUCING THE NEW TESTAMENT AND THE GREAT EIGHT WITNESSES

Christians' theology of revelation regarding the New Testament differs from Muslims' understanding of the Qur'an. Indeed, the twenty-seven New Testament books are written by eight different authors: Matthew, Mark, Luke, John, Paul, James, Peter, and Jude. This inquiry will furthermore refer to the collective group of New Testament writers as "The Great Eight Witnesses," or simply "The Great Eight." Christians believe the Holy Spirit moved upon these writers to write the exact words they wrote, even though their respective writings bear some stylistic and word selections particular to each author. Christians call this process the verbal plenary inspiration of the Bible by the Holy Spirit in which each word ("verbal") is fully ("plenary") inspired.

At the outset, Muslim readers will observe that the entire Holy Bible comprises sixty-six books written by approximately forty inspired authors over 1,500 years. The New Testament subset was written by the Great Eight during the 60 years after the ascension of the Lord Jesus Christ to heaven. The Qur'an, on the other hand, relies on one prophet prophesying over 23 years. These represent significant differences which impact both witness credibility, corroboration, and reliability.

The New Testament is organized into several sections. Positioned first are four biographies of the life of Jesus, written by the apostles Matthew and John, as well as those written by Mark and Luke. After the four Gospels follows an approximate thirty-five-year history of the early Christians, known as the Acts of the Apostles, also written by Luke. Following Acts come twenty-one teaching letters, known as epistles, which were addressed to either churches or individuals. At least thirteen of the epistles were written by Paul. John wrote three epistles, Peter wrote two, and James and Jude wrote one apiece. One epistle, known as the Epistle to the Hebrews, was unsigned. Even though the Church has received this important epistle as inspired and canonical, there has not been unanimous consensus on its authorship. Some churches believe it was written by Paul, though other possible writers have been nominated. The final book of the New Testament is known as the Revelation of Jesus to John, or simply as Revelation or The Apocalypse. This book utilizes apocalyptic imagery to describe the end of the age.

PAUL AND THE GREAT EIGHT

As stated in the previous chapter, Muslims frequently claim that Paul hijacked Christianity. The assertion states that Jesus presented himself as a mortal messenger of *tawhid*, similar to other prophets who came before him. Afterward, Paul changed those doctrines to what Christians now believe. Such a theory must therefore investigate Paul's contribution to the New Testament, which is the source of Christian doctrine.

The Greek New Testament is comprised of twenty-seven books containing 7,957 verses. Considering the verse count of Hebrews as unattributable to any one author, Luke wrote the most verses of any New Testament author. His two-part history, the Gospel of Luke, and the Acts of the Apostles, contain 2,158 verses. Paul's writings include 2,033 verses. John's writings rank third with 1,415 verses.

In summary, Paul authored one-quarter of the New Testament. Even if Paul was the author of Hebrews, that overall fraction does not change significantly. Three quarters of the New Testament were written by authors other than Paul.

Significantly, Paul did not write an account of the life of Jesus Christ. There is no "Gospel of Paul." It would seem if Paul was intent on hijacking or diverting Christianity, or leading Christians astray, he would have sought to produce a different life story of Jesus than the biography which Christians believe. Instead, Paul accepted the Gospel testimonies of Jesus which were already being widely circulated, including those of Luke and Mark, both of whom he traveled with, and both of whom he knew well.

The data presented thus far decrease the likelihood that Paul hijacked Christianity. Paul was a notable early Christian missionary and prominent theologian. His theological contribution perhaps rivals that of the apostle John as the most important in the New Testament. Yet by no means was Paul the overall leader of Christianity. The early church in Jerusalem, which was the headquarters of early Christianity, was led first by Peter, and then by James, the half-brother of Jesus. All these Christians—Paul, John, Peter, and James—as well as the other notable writers among the Great Eight, considered themselves nothing other than coworkers and servants of the Lord Jesus Christ.

Later, this research will focus on the beliefs Christians hold which contradict the standard Islamic narrative. Thus far, the data indicate that the New Testament was a broad-based book made up of twenty-seven documents claimed by Christians to be inspired. At least eight different authors contributed to the New Testament. Each writer contributed less than one-third of the overall content. The harmony of the Great Eight will be considered in upcoming chapters, as well as any disagreements they had.

BRIEF BIOGRAPHIES OF THE GREAT EIGHT

Matthew: Matthew was a Galilean Jewish tax collector. He was called by Jesus to be one of the twelve apostles. His Gospel, known as the Gospel of Matthew, quotes heavily from the Old Testament and therefore is thought to address Jewish readers more than did the other three Gospels. Matthew walked with Jesus during the three years of Jesus' public ministry. Matthew preached in Judea and other countries before he was martyred.

Mark, also known as John Mark: Mark was the author of the Gospel that bears his name, which is the shortest of the four Gospels. Mark wrote a fast-moving, action-packed account of Jesus' life which includes less of Jesus' sermon content than do the other three Gospels. However, there is significant content overlap in the Gospels of Matthew, Mark, and Luke, such that they are called as a group, "The Synoptic Gospels." Some scholars hold that the Gospel of Mark was the first Gospel written.

Though Mark was not one of the twelve original disciples, his Gospel includes a unique testimony of a young man who was following Jesus at the time of Jesus' arrest in the Garden of Gethsemane. That young man was seized, but quickly escaped (Mark 14:51–52). Many commentators consider this to have been Mark himself—since the other Gospel writers do not recount this incident—which would have placed him as a central witness during Jesus' last days on this earth.

Mark came from one of the early leading families who were following Jesus. When an angel miraculously sprung Peter from prison in Acts 12, he went immediately to the house of Mark's mother Mary, where a prayer meeting was occurring (Acts 12:12). Mark was also the cousin of the early leader Barnabas (Col 4:10), with whom he traveled as part of the first missionary team sent out from Antioch, which included Paul. Though Mark left this missionary trip for unknown reasons, he went on to establish the church in Alexandria, Egypt, where he preached against idolatry and was eventually martyred. Though Mark was not one of the original twelve, he is thought to have received much content about Jesus' life from Peter based on the close relationship indicated above.

Luke: Luke is thought to be the only non-Jewish writer of any New Testament book. He himself was a doctor (Col 4:14) and perhaps the most systematic researcher of any New Testament author. He addressed his Gospel and his accompanying Acts of the Apostles to "Theophilus," which means "lover of God." This name may have been applied generically to lovers of God or to a specific person who bore that name. Luke's Gospel begins with a statement that he "investigated everything carefully" based on the reports of "eyewitnesses" to the life of Christ (Luke 1:2–3). Luke also traveled in ministry with Paul, as indicated by the inclusive "we" narratives with which Luke describes several of Paul's travels in Acts.

John: The apostle John, not to be confused with John the Baptist (Yahya), was one of the original twelve apostles. He was part of Jesus' inner circle of three, along with Peter and John's brother James. In his Gospel, John writes about a disciple particularly beloved by Jesus (13:23). The language used by John in verses 21:20 and 21:24 indicate that the beloved disciple John writes about is in fact himself. Jesus also indicated his closeness to John when He entrusted the care of His mother Mary to John as He died on the cross (John 19:25–27). John stakes the credibility of his writings on his personal proximity to Jesus:

> What was from the beginning, what we have heard, what we have seen with our eyes, what we have looked at and touched with our hands, concerning the Word of Life— 2 and the life was manifested, and we have seen and testify and proclaim to you the eternal life, which was with the Father and was manifested to us— 3 what we have seen and heard we proclaim to you also, so that you too may have fellowship with us; and indeed our fellowship is with the Father, and with His Son Jesus Christ. (1 John 1:1–3)

John wrote the Gospel of John, as well as three epistles known as First John, Second John, and Third John. He also penned the Revelation while in exile at Patmos near the end of his life. Prior to that, he had ministered in Ephesus and was considered a pillar of the early church. John is thought to have been a young man during Jesus' earthly ministry. He likely outlived the other apostles. John's writings are considered to have been written last among the New Testament writings, in approximately AD 90, near the end of John's life.

Paul: The apostle Paul was born with the name Saul in Tarsus of modern-day Turkey. He was a Jewish Pharisee, later educated in Jerusalem under Gamaliel. Paul was a fierce persecutor of the early church, prior to a visitation from Jesus on the Road to Damascus. Luke narrates Jesus' encounter with Paul in Acts 9, as well as Paul's narration of these events in Acts 22 and 26. Paul provides an abundance of autobiographical information, as well as testimonies of his relationship with Christ, in many of his epistles.

Paul took three notable missionary journeys as chronicled in Acts. Indeed, he is the key Christian figure in Acts from chapters 13 through 28, at which time the narration ends with Paul in prison in Rome. His epistles constitute follow-up exhortations to the churches and individuals he encountered on these missionary journeys. Paul was martyred in Rome under Nero. Chapter 5 will examine in detail Paul's relationship to the early church and the Great Eight.

James: James, or Yaakov, was the half-brother of the Lord Jesus. He was born to Joseph and Mary, the mother of Jesus. He should not be confused with James the Son of Zebedee, one of the twelve apostles who was the brother of John the apostle and an early martyr. James the brother of the Lord Jesus is sometimes titled "James the Just," while the son of Zebedee is often called "James the Great."

James the Just authored the Epistle of James. He also became the leader of the mother church in the New Testament, located in Jerusalem. James was neither an original apostle nor one of the early believers in Jesus (see John 7:5). However, he rose to leadership in the early church. James arbitrated the settlement to controversies surrounding the reception of gentiles into Christ's kingdom. That event, known as the Jerusalem Council, is narrated by Luke in Acts 15, and is dated approximately AD 50. Having grown up with Jesus in the home of Mary and Joseph, James possessed a unique angle and intimate familiarity with the life of Jesus.

Peter: Simon Peter was an original disciple of Jesus and one of the inner three discipleship circle. Peter and his brother, the apostle Andrew, were Galilean fishermen before becoming leaders in the early church. Peter became the leader and spokesperson for the early church in Jerusalem. Acts 2–5 provide notable examples of Peter's leadership role in the early church, including his sermon on the Day of Pentecost. Peter served as spokesperson during legal entanglements with the Jewish leadership in Jerusalem.

Peter's ministry travels within Palestine are chronicled in Acts 9:32—11:18. He led what became known as the "Gentile Pentecost" at Cornelius' home in Caesarea (Acts 10). Peter is also connected to ministry in Samaria (Acts 8:14–23) and Antioch (Gal 2:11). He also traveled beyond the Levant. Peter is reported to have been martyred in Rome by Nero. Peter authored two epistles in the New Testament.

Jude: There are several people named Jude or Judas mentioned in the New Testament. This Jude, like James the Just, was a half-brother of the Lord Jesus, raised in the home of Mary and Joseph. Jude contributes a short epistle to the New Testament canon, consisting of a single chapter.

In summary, the Great Eight Witnesses include the following:

- Three of Jesus' original twelve disciples: Matthew, John, and Peter

- Two of Jesus' half-brothers: James and Jude

- Paul, the convert

- Luke, the gentile doctor, historian, and apostle

- Mark, the Gospel writer and missionary

The Great Eight provide a broad base from which a reliable record of Jesus' life and teaching can be derived. All of them lived at the time of Jesus, and at least five of them knew Him very well. Historians have contested the dates of some New Testament books and even the authorship of some of them. Had there only been one or two New Testament authors, then such contestations could prove devastating. However, three of the New Testament authors lived with Jesus for over three years, heard His words, saw His actions, and witnessed His crucifixion and resurrection.

Had Christianity been hijacked by any usurper, there were many credible voices which could have corrected this usurpation. The apostle John is widely thought to have written last. Based on his close relationship to Christ, John could have warned against emerging errors or usurpers. Indeed, John warned against an emerging heresy known as Gnosticism, yet he was the greatest defender among the Great Eight of Jesus' divinity. In conclusion, the Great Eight wrote down Jesus' words and actions in what would later be known as Christian orthodoxy, or "right-doctrine."

Nevertheless, the New Testament did not take its full and final form during the first Christian century. That would occur later, but long before the advent of Islam. Therefore, this study will next examine the bridges from the early Christians, including the Great Eight, to the time of New Testament canonization. Muslim scholars and thinkers will find this chain of transmission important to the inquiry into when, where, and how Christians may have gone astray.

Chapter 4

The Bridge from the Great Eight to New Testament Canonization

THIS INQUIRY HAS THUS far considered the possibility that early Christianity was hijacked, or at least that the main body of Christians was led astray. That straying into *shirk* (idolatry) would have manifested as a doctrinal change from Jesus' qur'anic portrayal of himself as a mortal messenger of *tawhid*. This qur'anic Jesus announced that a prophet named Ahmad would come after him. Since Christians believe that Jesus is divine, as well as being the Savior of humanity, some major straying must have occurred for the Islamic narrative to be true. Most Muslims believe Christians have strayed, but it is not altogether clear when, where, or how they went astray.

Muslims and Christians have interacted for fourteen centuries. Earlier chapters of this research have cited the Qur'an, Hadith, and various Islamic commentators regarding the question of Christians going astray. However, people in each generation are responsible for their own spiritual destiny. To my knowledge, the questions posed by this inquiry—questions vitally important for Muslims—have largely been left unaddressed in this generation.

The previous chapter introduced the Great Eight, those disciples of Jesus who penned the twenty-seven books of the New Testament. Four of those books are biographies, known as Gospels, or in Islamic parlance, *siras*, to describe that important life which is the center of the Christian faith. Earlier, this study revealed that the early Christian message spread very quickly—to India and all parts of the "known world" during the lives of those who had been personally taught by Jesus Himself. Had any major straying occurred, it must have occurred very early in that first generation.

For example, if all the disciples spread the message throughout the world that Jesus was the mortal messenger of *tawhid*, and only later some "heretics" began preaching that Jesus was divine, then the holders of that widespread message of Jesus and *tawhid* could have risen up to quash the later, errant message. In fact, evidence suggests that the orthodox Christian message was preached worldwide early on. This orthodox message became embedded within many different ethno-linguistic contexts. This inquiry therefore must now probe more deeply into the transmission of this orthodox Christian message—the message of the New Testament written about by the Great Eight.

These early disciples must have met and huddled together after Jesus ascended to heaven. During His "Last Supper" with the disciples, Jesus promised them: "These things I have spoken to you while abiding with you. But the Helper, the Holy Spirit, whom the Father will send in My name, He will teach you all things, and *bring to your remembrance all that I said to you*" (John 14:26–27, emphasis added). The twelve apostles were the leaders in the collective recollection of Jesus' words and deeds. They all witnessed them together over three years.

BRIDGE PERSONS

A significant period of church history drew to a close with the deaths of those who knew Jesus personally. John the apostle died last among the original twelve. This generation would pass the torch of Christian orthodoxy to a series of generations known variously as the Early Church Fathers, the Apostolic Fathers, or the Post-Apostolic Fathers.

John, writing late in his life, toward the conclusion of the first century, states that the core teaching (Greek, *didache*) was already established and well known. He warns of deceivers who do not hold to "the teaching" of the apostles. True believers should not allow them into the house of God—home churches—to preach their errant message:

> 7 For many deceivers have gone out into the world, those who do not acknowledge Jesus Christ as coming in the flesh. This is the deceiver and the antichrist. 8 Watch yourselves, that you do not lose what we have accomplished, but that you may receive a full reward. 9 Anyone who goes too far and does not abide in the *teaching of Christ*, does not have God; the one who abides in *the teaching*, he has both the Father and the Son. 10 If anyone comes to you and does not bring *this teaching*, do not receive him into your house, and do not give him a greeting; 11 for the one who gives him a greeting participates in his evil deeds. (2 John 7–11, emphasis added)

Clement

Peter and Paul ministered in Rome. Both were eventually martyred there by Nero between AD 64 and 67. Rome soon became a leading center of early Christianity. Rome boasted a Jewish community, and an early church. Clement became the lead pastor, or bishop, of the church at Rome from AD 88–98. He is thought to be the Clement mentioned by Paul in his epistle to the Philippians (4:3).

Clement wrote a non-canonical letter to the believers in Corinth—a church which still exhibited some of the problems with authority structures that Paul had addressed a generation earlier in his two canonical epistles to the Corinthians. This letter, the First Epistle of Clement, is dated at AD 96. Such a dating would place it shortly after all the New Testament writings were completed.

In the First Epistle of Clement, he urges the Corinthians to "Take up the epistle of the blessed Paul the Apostle" (47.1). Clement also alludes to the New Testament canonical letters Romans, Galatians, Ephesians, and Philippians. He quotes many phrases from the canonical Epistle to the Hebrews. This early writing shows that the New Testament documents were already in wide circulation and considered authoritative. Clement provides evidence that the churches knew what was happening in other churches. They were committed to holding each other accountable, thus making a widespread corruption, or *tahrif*, unlikely.

Clement wrote of God as Father, Son, and Holy Spirit. He described Jesus Christ as Lord:

> For Christ is of those who are humble-minded, and not of those who exalt themselves over His flock. Our Lord Jesus Christ, the Sceptre of the majesty of God, did not come in the pomp of pride or arrogance, although He might have done so, but in a lowly condition, as the Holy Spirit had declared regarding Him.[1]

Polycarp and Ignatius

The apostle John personally discipled two church leaders who would bridge the first and second centuries. Polycarp (AD 69–155) was the bishop of Smyrna (modern-day Izmir, Turkey). In his writings, Polycarp quotes sixty times from New Testament books, again showing that these books were in general circulation and considered to be Scripture. Polycarp followed in the footsteps of Jesus' original twelve disciples (except for Judas Iscariot and the apostle John) in dying as a martyr for the Lord Jesus Christ. Christianity was illegal in the Roman Empire until Constantine's Edict of Milan in AD 313. Thus, persecution was a very real possibility for these leaders. Scammers and deceivers rarely die for a lie. Polycarp, to the contrary, gave this testimony regarding his savior Jesus:

---

1. Keith, *First Clement*, 233.

Then he was brought forward, and great was the din as they heard that Polycarp was arrested. So he was brought before the Proconsul, who asked him if he was Polycarp. He said, "Yes," and the Proconsul tried to persuade him to deny the faith, urging, "Have respect to your old age," and the rest of it, according to the customary form, "Swear by the genius of Caesar; change your mind; say, "Away with the Atheists!" Then Polycarp looked with a stern countenance on the multitude of lawless heathen gathered in the stadium, and waved his hands at them, and looked up into heaven with a groan, and said, "Away with the Atheists." The Proconsul continued insisting and saying, "Swear, and I release you; curse Christ." And Polycarp said, "Eighty-six years have I served Him, and He has done me no wrong: how then can I blaspheme my King who saved me?"[2]

John the apostle discipled another key church leader, Ignatius, bishop of Antioch. Ignatius was martyred while traveling to Rome in the early second century. He also formed a human bridge between the first and second centuries. He challenged the heresies of his time, and frequently wrote pastoral letters to the churches.

Irenaeus

Irenaeus was a church leader born and raised in Smyrna while Polycarp ministered there. Irenaeus' life spanned AD 130–202. While the exact discipleship relationship between Polycarp and Irenaeus is not specified, the influence of Polycarp's teaching on him appears to have been strong.

When Irenaeus relocated to serve as a pastor in what is modern-day Lyon, France, he authored his famous work *Against Heresies*, dated approximately AD 180. This seminal book of the late second century largely rebukes Gnosticism, which taught that all flesh is evil and thus Jesus only appeared to come to the earth in human form. Gnostics taught that Jesus was an apparition or non-tangible being. Such a belief defies orthodox Christian doctrine.

2. Stevenson, *New Eusebius*, 21.

John the apostle also rebuked Gnosticism and its supposed secret knowledge in 1 John 4:1–3.

Students of church history may likewise confront the term "Docetism," which is similar to Gnosticism. Docetism stems from the Greek word *dokeo*, meaning "to appear." In Docetist theology, Jesus only appeared to visit the earth. Of course, this contradicts Islamic theology also. Docetism relies on the Greek philosophical tenet of idealism or essentialism—that the pure or ideal form of a thing is its intangible "essence." Since both Islam and orthodox Christianity teach that Jesus had a fleshly body, the prospect that Gnosticism or Docetism comprised the original message of Christ from which Christians strayed seems implausible. Nevertheless, Irenaeus was compelled to confront and expose their heretical teachings.

Irenaeus describes the four Gospels in circulation:

> Matthew also issued a written Gospel among the Hebrews in their own dialect, while Peter and Paul were preaching at Rome, and laying the foundations of the Church. After their departure, Mark, the disciple and interpreter of Peter, did also hand down to us in writing what had been preached by Peter. Luke also, the companion of Paul, recorded in a book the Gospel preached by him. Afterwards, John, the disciple of the Lord, who also had leaned upon His breast, did himself publish a Gospel during his residence at Ephesus in Asia.[3]

Irenaeus also rebuked a Jewish legalistic sect, the "Ebionites." The sect promoted salvation by good deeds; keeping the Mosaic law; the non-divinity of Messiah Jesus; the rejection of the virgin birth of Christ; and the rejection of the New Testament except for portions of Matthew's Gospel. Notably, the apostle Matthew was never reported to endorse this heresy. Though it did not reach its full fruition until the second century, some seeds of the problem are evident in Acts 21:20 and in Paul's epistle to the Galatians. The early church always considered these legalistic emanations as heresies and threats to orthodoxy. Irenaeus condemned the Ebionites

3. Irenaeus, *Ag. Her.* 3.1.1.

in *Against Heresies*. Muslim readers will be able to evaluate whether such a heresy could have been the original teaching of Jesus as this inquiry moves forward; Ebionism denies the virgin birth of Christ which Islam embraces. Yet, the chain from John to Polycarp to Irenaeus appears unbroken relationally and theologically.

Origen

The early church leader Origen wrote a commentary on the entire Gospel of Matthew in AD 246–48. He also published commentaries on the Gospel of John and the book of Romans.[4] Such writings indicate these books were in wide circulation and considered authoritative for Christians. As such, Christians would have had an interest in reading commentaries on these Scriptures.

By the middle of the third century, orthodox Christianity had grown widely in all directions from Jerusalem. The message was established in various parts of Europe, Africa, the Middle East, and Asia. New Testament books had been translated into multiple languages; their retraction would have posed an insurmountable challenge. By this time, it would have proven difficult for a major campaign of misguidance to successfully gain traction in a way that could sidetrack the entire movement.

THE EARLY MANUSCRIPTS

The original inspired twenty-seven New Testament manuscripts (handwritten) penned by the Great Eight are not now in the possession of the church. It is extremely unlikely they will be found, though they were not lost. As widely circulated manuscripts read by the churches, they no doubt wore out and wore through, and were replaced by newly copied manuscripts. In that copying process, some scribal errors occurred. Christians readily concede this point. The multiplicity and preponderance of the number of

4. Patrick, *Origen's Commentary*, 411.

manuscripts—over 5,000 Greek manuscripts[5]—makes it relatively easy to see where copyist errors occurred in the manuscripts.

This section traces the manuscript chain. A full academic treatment of textual transmission of the New Testament manuscripts could fill many books. This short book is not designed for that purpose. Instead, the inquiry at hand is to assist Muslim scholars and thinkers in evaluating the Islamic claim that Christians have gone astray. If Christians have been led astray, ample historical evidence should exist to substantiate that thesis, particularly regarding the New Testament chain of transmission. If, on the other hand, the Great Eight faithfully described what Jesus taught, and those writings have been faithfully passed on, then the Islamic accusation is still left to be corroborated.

The Rylands 52 papyrus from John's Gospel constitutes the earliest manuscript "fragment" of the Greek New Testament. This manuscript dates to AD 130. This fragment demonstrates that the Gospel of John penetrated to Egypt within a generation of its writing. The Bodmer Papyrus collection dates from the second half of the second century (AD 150–200) and includes the Gospel of Luke, the Gospel of John, the Epistle of Jude, and 1 and 2 Peter.

Complete Greek New Testaments exist and can be seen by interested parties today. These include the Codex Sinaiticus, found at Mount Sinai, and the Codex Vaticanus. Both date from AD 325–50. I have seen the former where it is displayed at the British Library in London. These manuscripts predate Islam by three centuries.

Athanasius of Alexandria provided the earliest complete list of the twenty-seven New Testament books, in 367. That canon was adopted at the Council of Carthage in AD 397. The Council participants did not confer initial Scriptural authority on these twenty-seven books. Rather, they were stating which books they found authoritative, and which had *already* been considered authoritative by the early church. Books attained scriptural authority

---

5. Though Jesus most likely spoke to his disciples in the semitic language Aramaic, with various Hebrew religious terms, Koine Greek was widely understood in Galilee. As the "lingua franca" of its day, the Great Eight wrote in Koine Greek.

based on apostolic connections, as well as the fact that the books were widely read and widely accepted and used in worship. The fact that they were used widely before canonization means that it would have been impossible to have gathered all the manuscripts together, produced a replacement with innovations, and redistributed it. Christians had no governmental power to even attempt such an endeavor until the fourth century.

Athanasius also countered the teaching of Arius, who stated that the Son of God was not equal to the Father in nature. Regarding the Son, Arius stated, "There was a time when he was not; for the Son is a creature and a work."[6] He held that the Son was created, in contradiction to John 1:3, which states that Jesus was Himself the Creator. Arius held that Jesus was a lesser god, or demi-god.[7] Thus, he was criticized as a polytheist, and therefore must be considered un-Islamic. Since Arius lived and taught three centuries after Christ, it is unlikely that he could have propagated the proto-Christian teaching from which the main body of Christians went astray.

CONCLUSION

Based on these brief descriptions, Muslim scholars and thinkers will be able to ponder any credible scenario in which Jesus' movement could have been hijacked. If Christians had gone astray *en masse*, it would likely have had to occurred very early in the movement. Various heresies and splinter groups indeed emerged. Gnosticism was likely present at the time of Christ, though it is an un-Islamic teaching. Ebionism, an extreme form of Jewish legalism, emerged after the time of Christ. Yet, Ebionites rejected the virgin birth, which Islam upholds. Other pseudo-Christian heresies emerged later. Muslim scholars and thinkers will be able to evaluate the possibility that any of these heresies were indeed the teaching of Jesus from which the main body of Christians

6. Athanasius, *Deposition of Arius*, 336.

7. Encyclopædia Britannica, "Arianism."

may have strayed. They will also be able to judge the plausibility of the Islamic doctrine of *tahrif*—the corruption of pre-qur'anic Scriptures.

Before addressing the specific doctrines of Christian orthodoxy which are anti-qur'anic, this study will focus on the relationship of the apostle Paul to the other members of the Great Eight and to the wider early church. As mentioned above, Paul is often portrayed as the culprit who hijacked or diverted Christianity. Scholarly Muslim thinkers therefore do well to investigate Paul's relationships with other early church leaders.

Chapter 5

The Relationships between Paul and the Other Early Church Leaders

THE STANDARD ISLAMIC NARRATIVE requires that Christians went astray. Sura 1:7 refers to a group who have strayed from *as-Sirat al-Mustaqeem*. The prophet of Islam identified these as *an-Nasara*, Christians. Muslim commentators, *al-mufassiruun*, have confirmed this Islamic tenet. Indeed, since Islam teaches that Jesus was a mortal messenger of *tawhid*, and since Christians believe that Jesus is Lord, God, and Savior, a major straying must have taken place on the part of Christians for the Islamic narrative to be true.

Muslim scholars and thinkers will naturally want to know who led the Christians astray, how they were led astray, and when they were led astray. Interfaith dialog demands some answers to these questions. Nevertheless, little in the way of deep investigation has been performed or spoken about regarding these pressing issues. At least in our generation, this discussion does not feature in interfaith dialog between Christians and Muslims.

For the standard Islamic narrative to be true it is not necessary that the apostle Paul be the guilty party in leading Christians astray. However, there are readily available reasons why Muslims have identified him as a leading candidate. (Indeed, Paul has no shortage of critics in Jewish, Christian, and academic circles, either.)

First, Paul did not number among the original twelve disciples who walked with Jesus for three years. Thus, he might have been more likely to stray from Jesus' teaching and life example since he was not present to observe that sacred history. Second, Paul was a convert into the Jesus movement. Thus, it is possible to hypothesize that he did not share the ethos and beliefs of others who had been in the movement longer. Third, Paul had several notable disagreements with other early church leaders, such as Peter and Barnabas, who were pillars of the early church. Any of these data points could provide a basis for the theory that Paul led Christians astray from Jesus' message of *tawhid* and Christ's self-perception as a mortal prophet. These claims will be investigated below.

PAUL AND BARNABAS

After Paul's conversion to Christ on the road to Damascus, he journeyed to Jerusalem. The believers there were initially afraid of him, based on his reputation as a persecutor of Christians (Acts 9:26). However, Barnabas was convinced that Paul's conversion was sincere, and he vouched for Paul before the other church leaders. Thereafter, Paul returned to his hometown of Tarsus.

When Christian witnesses eventually established a church in Antioch—a major city of antiquity near the modern-day border of Syria and Turkey—it was comprised of Jewish and gentile adherents. When news of this development reached the Jerusalem church, they sent Barnabas to Antioch to assist the new work (Acts 11:22). Most likely they chose him since he had a gifting in spiritual encouragement. Indeed, his given name was Joseph; church leaders dubbed him "Barnabas," a nickname that meant "Son of Encouragement." As Barnabas encouraged Paul, so he encouraged the Antiochenes.

Barnabas knew that Paul had a calling to minister among gentiles (Acts 9:15). So, when Barnabas witnessed the development of the ministry in Antioch, he left Antioch to travel to Tarsus to look for Paul, who at this time was still being called by his given name, Saul (Acts 11:25–26). Barnabas returned with Paul to Antioch where they together taught the new followers of Christ for one year. It was at Antioch that the followers of Jesus were first called "Christians" and Saul became known as "Paul."

The Antiochene church then sent out a missionary team which included Barnabas, Paul, and Mark. The team's initial destination was Cyprus, the home of Barnabas. After preaching in Salamis, Paphos, and throughout the island, the team embarked on a tour of the Galatian region of Asia Minor. However, Mark left the team for some reason which Luke does not report (Acts 13:13). Paul and Barnabas concluded a tour of Asia Minor in which they preached, worked miracles, and planted several churches.

Later, after the Jerusalem Council of Acts 15, Paul suggested to Barnabas that they make a return tour of Asia Minor to strengthen the new churches and disciples of Christ. Barnabas was willing to do so, but wanted to take along with them Mark, who happened to be his cousin. Paul refused, so they parted ways, forming two teams. Luke recounts the incident as follows in Acts 15:36–41:

> 36 After some days Paul said to Barnabas, "Let us return and visit the brethren in every city in which we proclaimed the word of the Lord, and see how they are." 37 Barnabas wanted to take John, called Mark, along with them also. 38 But Paul kept insisting that they should not take him along who had deserted them in Pamphylia and had not gone with them to the work. 39 And there occurred such a sharp disagreement that they separated from one another, and Barnabas took Mark with him and sailed away to Cyprus. 40 But Paul chose Silas and left, being committed by the brethren to the grace of the Lord. 41 And he was traveling through Syria and Cilicia, strengthening the churches.

In the end, two teams were formed. Later, Paul wrote to the church at Colossae that they should welcome Mark if he comes to visit them (Col 4:10). In 2 Tim 4:11, Paul wrote at the end of his life that Mark "is useful to me for service." Paul also commends Mark in his letter to Philemon (v. 24). Apparently, he and Mark reconciled their relationship. Mark proceeded with a successful ministry career, planting the church in Egypt and writing the second canonical Gospel.

Muslims scholars and thinkers may recall the parting of the ways of Ali bin Abu Talib from Abu Bakr and the main group of the umma in the early days of Islam. Sometimes leaders choose to part ways. In the case of Barnabas and Paul, they ministered together extensively over several years. It is impossible they could have done so if they differed regarding their core beliefs. Their split was only what could be called a "personnel decision" over the appointment or re-instatement of a member of their missionary team.

Insinuations exist that Paul hijacked Christianity and that Barnabas was a true preacher of *tawhid*. This line of thinking maintains that the Gospel of Barnabas is the true account of Jesus' life, while the canonical Gospels are false. Muslims also need to consider that Jesus declares in the Gospel of Barnabas that he is not *al-Masih* (The Messiah).[1] Therefore, the Gospel of Barnabas makes Jesus out to be a liar in relation to Islamic doctrine. Further, no early manuscripts of that document exist; the earliest manuscripts date only from the fourteenth to seventeenth centuries. Scholars consider the Gospel of Barnabas a late forgery which usurps the name of Barnabas.

In conclusion, Barnabas and Paul were very close associates who preached together in multiple cities. They taught together in Antioch for a year. They disagreed over a personnel appointment. There is no evidence that either one changed their core beliefs from orthodox Christian beliefs or sought to change the beliefs of the main body of Christians.

---

1. Ragg and Ragg, *Gospel of Barnabas*, 82:3, 96:2–3, 97:1, 97:6.

PAUL AND PETER

The two great early Christian leaders were united in martyrdom in Rome under Nero. This inquiry considers their relationship during their respective lives. One notable dispute occurred between the two, also in Antioch.

A backdrop to this interaction will inform the interpretation of the conflict in Antioch reported below. The early Christians were Jews who kept a kosher diet, similar to the Islamic *halal* requirement. Jews were forbidden to eat pork, and certain other animals. Gentiles were not subject to these dietary laws. Fellowship between the two groups proved difficult, since fellowship usually involved eating together. Peter experienced a profound vision prior to the "gentile Pentecost" at the home of a gentile military commander named Cornelius. Luke describes this event in Acts 10:9–16:

> On the next day, as they were on their way and approaching the city, Peter went up on the housetop about the sixth hour to pray. 10 But he became hungry and was desiring to eat; but while they were making preparations, he fell into a trance; 11 and he saw the sky opened up, and an object like a great sheet coming down, lowered by four corners to the ground, 12 and there were in it all kinds of four-footed animals and crawling creatures of the earth and birds of the air. 13 A voice came to him, "Get up, Peter, kill and eat!" 14 But Peter said, "By no means, Lord, for I have never eaten anything unholy and unclean." 15 Again a voice came to him a second time, "What God has cleansed, no longer consider unholy." 16 This happened three times, and immediately the object was taken up into the sky.

Muslim readers may be reminded of Sura Ma'ida (The Table Spread), Q5:112–14, which contains some similarities to this narrative. Based on this vision, Peter became a champion of open fellowship with gentiles. This position required him to no longer abide by Jewish kosher laws, a position the wider church would later adopt. However, some Jewish Christians were very hesitant to abandon kosher laws and even Jewish circumcision rites. These came into conflict with both Peter (see Acts 11:3) and Paul.

However, on one occasion in Antioch, Peter waffled in his practice of open fellowship and eating with gentiles. When conservative brethren from Judea visited Antioch, Peter changed his practice and withdrew from eating with the gentiles. Paul rebuked and corrected Peter, also known as Cephas. Paul writes in Gal 2:11–14:

> When Cephas came to Antioch, I opposed him to his face, because he stood condemned. 12 For prior to the coming of certain men from James, he used to eat with the Gentiles; but when they came, he began to withdraw and hold himself aloof, fearing the party of the circumcision. 13 The rest of the Jews joined him in hypocrisy, with the result that even Barnabas was carried away by their hypocrisy. 14 But when I saw that they were not straightforward about the truth of the gospel, I said to Cephas in the presence of all, "If you, being a Jew, live like the Gentiles and not like the Jews, how is it that you compel the Gentiles to live like Jews?"

Peter deserved the rebuke he received from Paul. Barnabas also received censure. Nevertheless, the issue being considered at that time was dietary laws, and secondarily, circumcision. These issues greatly impacted the inclusion of the gentiles into the church. Yet, these do not constitute the central issues to Christian orthodoxy being discussed among Christians and Muslims. Nor are they issues that impact the inquiry into whether Jesus Christ portrayed himself as a mortal messenger of *tawhid*, or whether He portrayed Himself as Lord, God, and Savior.

Importantly, when Peter later wrote his epistles, he commended Paul to the wider church, describing him as "beloved." This is an important commendation, though Peter concedes that some of Paul's writings were complicated:

> Therefore, beloved, since you look for these things, be diligent to be found by Him in peace, spotless and blameless, 15 and regard the patience of our Lord as salvation;

> just as also our *beloved brother Paul*, according to the
> wisdom given him, wrote to you, 16 as also in all his let-
> ters, speaking in them of these things, in which are some
> things hard to understand, which the untaught and un-
> stable distort, as they do also the rest of the Scriptures, to
> their own destruction. (2 Pet 3:14–16, emphasis added)

In this canonical epistle, Peter, one of the Great Eight, calls Paul "beloved" and commends his letters (epistles) to the wider church. Had Peter been concerned that Paul was hijacking Christianity or leading Christians astray, he would rather have issued dire warnings about Paul. Instead, he commended Paul and castigated those who distorted Paul's teaching. The main area of contention between Paul and some Jewish believers in Christ from Judea surrounded the introduction of the gentiles in the body of Christ, which is the church. Paul rejected circumcision and dietary mandates, since gentiles did not practice these things previously. Paul reasoned that if the gentiles adopted these legal rites as good deeds, they would trust in them for salvation rather than trusting in what Christ had accomplished on the cross. The gentiles would furthermore place themselves under the requirement of fulfilling the whole Mosaic law—a requirement they were not able to fulfill. Paul clearly articulates his position in his teaching epistle to the Galatians.

PAUL AND OTHER CHURCH LEADERS

James assumed the leadership of the Jerusalem Church after Peter began to travel more extensively to other areas. James was one of the Great Eight. He arbitrated the Jerusalem Council controversy over dietary issues and Gentile uncleanness. As he gave a ruling to the Council, James, the brother of the Lord Jesus, also called Paul "beloved" in a letter that would announce the Council's ruling:

> Then it seemed good to the apostles and the elders, with
> the whole church, to choose men from among them to
> send to Antioch with Paul and Barnabas—Judas called

Barsabbas, and Silas, leading men among the brethren, 23 and they sent this letter by them,

"The apostles and the brethren who are elders, to the brethren in Antioch and Syria and Cilicia who are from the Gentiles: Greetings.

24 Since we have heard that some of our number to whom we gave no instruction have disturbed you with their words, unsettling your souls, 25 it seemed good to us, having become of one mind, to select men to send to you with our *beloved Barnabas and Paul*, 26 men who have risked their lives for the name of our Lord Jesus Christ. 27 Therefore we have sent Judas and Silas, who themselves will also report the same things by word of mouth." (Acts 15:22–27, emphasis added)

The Jerusalem Council occurred approximately twenty years into the early church era. The Second Epistle of Peter was written sometime after that. Peter and James, both members of the Great Eight, and the two most prominent leaders of the early mother church in Jerusalem, commended Paul as "beloved." Had he been trying to hijack their movement, or lead their flock astray, they certainly would not have praised him in this manner.

PAUL'S SKIRMISHES WITH OTHER CHRISTIANS

Throughout the duration of Paul's ministry, the Jewish groups that rejected Jesus as Messiah sought to kill Paul. However, they were unsuccessful. They viewed him as a traitor and an apostate.

Paul also experienced differences of opinion with some of the early Christians. In most cases, this was based on misrepresentations of Paul's position regarding the abandonment of the Mosaic law, circumcision, and Jewish dietary laws. Acts 21:21 describes such an encounter which took place in Jerusalem, where emphasis on Jewish laws was more strident.

Paul also came into conflict with those who spread negative comments about him in Corinth. Paul planted the church in Corinth during his second missionary journey, as narrated in Acts

18. However, the church was beset by divisions, which Paul addressed in his first canonical letter to the church. Later, unnamed "super-apostles" came to Corinth slighting and disrespecting Paul (2 Cor 11:5). They hoped they could weaken the church's love for its founder, and peel off members to themselves. They insulted Paul as being a poor speaker and of unimpressive persona. Most likely these false teachers or super-apostles were jealous and self-centered. No evidence exists that they contested Paul over Christian orthodoxy, or the issues central to Jesus, *tawhid*, or Trinity. Divisions and insubordination continued to plague the Corinthian church for decades to the extent that Clement in Rome would later send them his corrective epistle.

CONCLUSION

If, as Ahmed Deedat contends, Paul diverted the Jesus movement and indeed founded Christianity, that would have been a surprise to Peter, James, Barnabas, and the other leaders of the early church. These leaders considered Paul a beloved brother and colaborer. If Paul was leading people astray, these leaders must have been leading them astray also. Instead, the evidence indicates that Paul was one of the Great Eight who, along with early church leaders such as Barnabas, promoted what would become known as Christian orthodoxy. It is to these major doctrines, and how they were treated by the Great Eight, that this study now turns.

PART III

An Inquiry into the Reliability of the Portrayal of the Lord Jesus' Life and Teaching as Represented in the New Testament

Chapter 6

Belief in a Personal, Loving God

THIS CHAPTER MARKS A turning point in our study. Earlier chapters addressed the general Islamic claim that Christians have gone astray by committing *shirk*. Since this straying is essential to the Islamic narrative, Muslims must identify when, where, and how Christians actually went astray.

Part III provides a deeper exploration into the doctrines of Christian orthodoxy which may be considered un-Islamic or anti-qur'anic. These may not be the only biblical doctrines which are contrary to Islam, but they include the main ones. One important issue that will not be considered directly is the nature of human beings—are humans inherently sinful by nature? Neither will this study delve into the important comparative study of the source of evil. Time and space simply will not allow for a complete examination of all theological divergences (or convergences) between Christianity and Islam.

Nevertheless, four key doctrines will be considered. By them, this inquiry will be delimited. The four specific doctrines to be examined will be the following:

- Chapter 6: Belief in a Personal, Loving God
- Chapter 7: Belief in the Divinity of Jesus

- Chapter 8: Belief in the Triune God

- Chapter 9: Belief in Salvation by Faith

The methodology of this research is to probe the twenty-seven New Testament books, written by the Great Eight Witnesses, including the book of Hebrews, to ascertain the breadth and depth of support for these doctrines. New Testament content which is recurring and broad-based will provide greater support for the doctrines above. Should any doctrine be advanced only by one author, such as by Paul for example, more rationale may exist for the argument that Christians have strayed in adopting such a doctrine. For these reasons, the New Testament content below does not constitute an exhaustive treatment of support for any of the doctrines, yet it seeks to be a fair treatment. I will include and reflect upon New Testament material that seems to contradict orthodox Christian doctrine. Muslims, by reading the New Testament, should experience little difficulty in discovering the teachings of orthodox Christianity.

A NOTE ON ORTHODOXY AND THE BRANCHES OF CHRISTIANITY

Muslim scholars and thinkers will likely have read or viewed material on comparative religions. This content typically includes material on theological convergence—how Christianity and Islam are similar—as well as theological divergence—how Christianity and Islam are different. This inquiry focuses on theological divergence.

An important qualifier in addressing whether Christians have gone astray may be to ask, "Which Christians?" The phrase "orthodox Christianity" has been utilized widely in this book. This may be confusing, since specific churches exist whose names include the term "Orthodox," such as the Greek Orthodox Church, or the Coptic Orthodox Church of Egypt.

As mentioned above, "orthodox" is a compound word meaning "right doctrine." In Arabic, orthodoxy is translated as *mustaqeem ra'i*, or Straight View, which features the same adjective used in *as-Sirat al-Mustaqeem*, the Straight Path. For simplicity, I will follow the standard practice of using lowercase for orthodoxy when it refers generally to the "right-doctrine" of Christians. When referring to the Orthodox Church or specific churches in this branch, I will use capitalization.

Christianity has three main branches: Catholic, Orthodox, and Protestant. While heated theological debates have existed among the branches on various topics, all branches historically adhere to the beliefs on the four major doctrines which will be detailed below. The final point—Salvation by Faith—generates the most interpretive tension among the branches. Chapter 9 will consider this topic, including how the grace of God in Christ is appropriated to the believers. Nevertheless, all branches of orthodox Christianity hold the same basic theology and Christology. This should not be surprising, to the extent the branches derive their teachings from the same holy book, the Holy Bible, in general, and the New Testament, in particular.

BELIEF IN A PERSONAL, LOVING GOD

Christianity and Islam hold in common many beliefs about the Almighty. Both religions teach that God alone dwelt in eternity past. He is the unique and only Creator. He is all-powerful. Only He will judge all souls on the Day of Judgment, *al-Yom ad-Din*.

Studies of comparative religion often focus on the Christian doctrine of Trinity versus the Islamic doctrine of *tawhid*. Yet, this inquiry warrants a preliminary discussion regarding the nature of God and His relationship to people. This chapter is positioned at this juncture because it provides a platform for the subsequent doctrines which build upon it.

The four doctrines under consideration flow from roots in the Old Testament. Indeed, the Great Eight and the other early Christians had as their Bible the Old Testament only. They themselves would provide the New Testament.

Muslims who read the Bible may be amazed—as I was—to open the first page of the Old Testament in Genesis which reads:

> Then God said, "Let Us make man in Our image, accord-
> ing to Our likeness; and let them rule over the fish of
> the sea and over the birds of the sky and over the cattle
> and over all the earth, and over every creeping thing that
> creeps on the earth." 27 God created man in His own
> image, in the image of God He created him; male and
> female He created them. (Gen 1:26-27)

Though Allah in the Qur'an often speaks in the "Royal We," two major points of emphasis spring from this first book of Moses, which is the first book of the Torah. First, the God of the Bible speaks of Himself as a pluralized unity rather than an absolute unity. Second, God created people—men and women—in His own image.

This chapter considers the second point. Since God created human beings in His image, then God's nature must be personal. He speaks and interacts with people in a relational way. Later discussions on the Fatherhood of God and the Sonship of Christ flow from the relational and familial nature of God presented by Moses at the outset of the Old Testament.

The Qur'an, on the other hand, presents the Almighty as impersonal. Therefore, He does not communicate directly with humans. Islamic doctrine states unequivocally that the prophet of Islam received his messages from the Angel Gabriel, who was an intermediary between Allah and man. As this chapter unfolds, biblical data will indicate that God's nature is loving. At this point, the Great Eight will speak to the doctrine of a Personal, Loving God.

Matthew: This disciple of Jesus records several important statements of Jesus Christ regarding the personal, loving God. First, Matthew reports Jesus as saying: "I say to you, love your enemies and pray for those who persecute you, so that you may be sons of your Father who is in heaven" (Matt 5:43–44).[1] By this statement, Jesus instructed His disciples that the Heavenly Father loves His enemies. Believers must not simply love and pray for their friends,

---

1. Some parallel passages will be noted, especially in the Synoptic Gospels, Matthew, Mark, and Luke. For a parallel reference to this passage from Matthew, see Luke 6:35–36.

but also for their enemies. Such an attitude, says Jesus, reflects the character of God.

Second, Jesus states that the Heavenly Father intends to provide good gifts to people: "If you then, being evil, know how to give good gifts to your children, how much more will your Father who is in heaven give what is good to those who ask Him!" (Matt 7:11).[2] In these two points, Jesus taught that God is fatherly in nature; He loves His enemies and gives good gifts to humans, even though we are evil. Muslims who read the Bible will quickly note points of theological divergence between the Bible and the Qur'an.

John:[3] In his Gospel, John captures a number of statements from Jesus that reflect the loving, personal nature of God. In a passage that will be considered in the next chapter on the divinity of Jesus, John narrates regarding believers in Christ: "As many as received Him, to them He gave the right to become children of God, even to those who believe in His name" (John 1:12). In the prior verse, John states that Jesus faced much rejection (v. 11), yet those who believed in Christ received the right or power to be children of God. John repeats this theme in the first of his teaching epistles: "See how great a love the Father has bestowed on us, that we would be called children of God; and such we are" (1 John 3:1).

Later this inquiry will consider the meaning of Jesus' title, "The Son of God." Since confusion may exist in the minds of Muslim readers regarding these verses—Matt 5:44, John 1:12, and 1 John 3:1—a brief explanation is warranted. A clear demarcation exists between people and God. No person can ever become God. However, when God grants spiritual rebirth and new life to humans, as will be described in chapter 9, these men, women, and children enter into a spiritual relationship with God as their Heavenly Father. This is what Matthew and John mean when they

---

2. Parallel reference: Luke 11:13.

3. The ordering of the four Gospels is Matthew, Mark, Luke, and John. Since Luke also authored the early church history known as the *Acts of the Apostles*, I have placed John before Luke, so that Luke and Acts can be considered consecutively.

speak of mortal humans becoming children of God. They describe a spiritual relationship.

Jesus Christ cannot be classified the same way. As will be explored below, the Son of God existed in eternity past as God, and later took on flesh to visit this earth in the form of a person. Jesus' advent into this world occurred 2,000 years ago when He was born of His virgin mother Mary.

John elaborates further about the loving nature of God, recording Jesus' words in what is commonly cited as the most famous verse of the Bible: "For God so loved the world, that He gave His only begotten Son, that whoever believes in Him shall not perish, but have eternal life" (John 3:16). As in 1 John 3:1, John describes the love of God in a superlative sense. God lavishes that love upon unworthy human beings.

John uniquely captures some statements of Jesus from His "Last Supper" with His disciples. That lavish, personal, unconditional, other-centered love of God, known in Greek as *agape*, is meant to be shared among believers. Jesus states: "A new commandment I give to you, that you love one another, even as I have loved you, that you also love one another" (John 13:34). Muslim readers may assess this personal relationship between the Creator of all people and the people themselves to be different than is found in Islam.

John recounts a confrontation in which the Jewish religious leaders who opposed Jesus stated their clear belief that God speaks to people: "We know that God has spoken to Moses, but as for this man [Jesus], we do not know where He is from" (John 9:29). As a young man who was raised Muslim, this was one of the first points in the Bible which arrested my attention—God spoke directly to people.

In his first epistle, John states that God by His nature is love: "Beloved, let us love one another, for love is from God; and everyone who loves is born of God and knows God. The one who does not love does not know God, for God is love" (1 John 4:7–8). "God is love" is not an abstract concept. Love requires the Lover, the Beloved, and the love that flows between them. Such an understanding provides the foundation for understanding the nature of the Triune God, which we will explore in chapter 8.

Luke: In the third Gospel, Luke provides historical data regarding the births of John the Baptist and Jesus Christ. Luke narrates the Angel Gabriel's visit to the Virgin Mary, announcing she will give birth to Jesus, the Savior. Gabriel exclaims to Mary, "Greetings, favored one! The Lord is with you" (Luke 1:28). Mary exults in reply regarding her personal relationship to God, her Savior: "My soul exalts the Lord; and my spirit has rejoiced in God my Savior!" (Luke 1:46–47). While Mary enjoys respect and renown as the only woman named in the Qur'an, her personal relationship to God described here is unique to the Bible.

Luke 15 features several parables Jesus taught regarding lost things. The chapter closes with the Parable of the Prodigal Son. That wayward son squandered his inheritance through sinful living. He ultimately found himself without friends or money, eating scraps among unclean pigs. At that point, he decided to return to his own father, whom he had shamed. "So he got up and came to his father. But while he was still a long way off, his father saw him and felt compassion for him, and ran and embraced him and kissed him" (Luke 15:20). The father demonstrates his compassion by running toward his long-lost son. He gave him a loving embrace. In this parable, Jesus compares this compassionate father to the Heavenly Father who loves sinful people.

In the Acts of the Apostles, Luke shares another instructive example in this topic area. As Paul preached at Pisidian Antioch in Acts 13:22, he spoke about God's view of King David, "I have found David son of Jesse a man after my own heart." Though David committed serious sins during his life, including murder and adultery, he was a worshipper of God. Muslims and Christians agree that the Psalmist David was a worshipper of God.

Indeed, the Old Testament features God's approval of David's heart attitude. God commissioned the prophet Samuel to anoint the next king of Israel. The Lord rejected David's brothers, though the eldest presented a formidable physical stature. God said to Samuel: "Do not look at his appearance or at the height of his stature, because I have rejected him; for God sees not as man sees, for man looks at the outward appearance, but the Lord looks at the heart" (1 Sam 16:7). God approved David and anointed him on the basis of the intention of his heart to worship God.

Paul: In his teaching letters, Paul corroborated the other New Testament writers in painting a picture of the personal, paternal love of God which qualifies as un-Islamic. Paul wrote to the Christians at Rome: "You have not received a spirit of slavery leading to fear again, but you have received a spirit of adoption as sons by which we cry out, "Abba! Father!" (Rom 8:15). The Aramaic phrase *Abba* is a cognate of the same term in Arabic. It can be thought of in English as "Daddy!"

Paul reiterates the nature of the love of God later in the same chapter:

> For I am convinced that neither death, nor life, nor angels, nor principalities, nor things present, nor things to come, nor powers, nor height, nor depth, nor any other created thing, will be able to separate us from the love of God, which is in Christ Jesus our Lord. (Rom 8:38–39)

Importantly, no created thing—including Satan or demons—can separate believers from the love of God in Christ Jesus the Lord. In his second letter to the church at Corinth, Paul refers to God as "the God of all comfort" (2 Cor 1:3). To the church at Ephesus, Paul wrote about the "kind intention of God's will" (see Eph 1:5, 9). Overall, Paul writes with comparable theological content to the other New Testament writers regarding the personal, loving nature of God.

Hebrews: Although no consensus exists regarding the authorship of Hebrews, Christians have always included it in the New Testament canon. This book corroborates earlier passages about God speaking to people: "God, after He spoke long ago to the fathers in the prophets in many portions and in many ways, in these last days has spoken to us in His Son" (Heb 1:1–2a).

James: The half-brother of Jesus became an early leader of the Jerusalem Church. He provides a poetic interpretation to the loving nature of God: "Every good thing given and every perfect gift is from above, coming down from the Father of lights, with whom there is no variation or shifting shadow" (Jas 1:17). James testifies both to the absolute faithfulness and the gift-giving nature of God.

Peter: The prominent apostle and disciple of Jesus wrote two epistles. In the first, he describes the great love of God for His people: "You are a chosen race, a royal priesthood, a holy nation, a people for God's own possession, so that you may proclaim the excellencies of Him who has called you out of darkness into His marvelous light" (1 Pet 2:9). God actually possesses, encompasses, and lovingly envelopes the people who have stepped into this marvelous light.

In his second epistle, Peter repeats the earlier theme of God speaking directly to people—in this case prophets who received inspired messages from God: "Know this first of all, that no prophecy of Scripture is a matter of one's own interpretation, for no prophecy was ever made by an act of human will, but men moved by the Holy Spirit spoke from God" (2 Pet 1:20–21). This passage proves instructive for Muslims who seek to understand the biblical view of prophethood and revelation, as well as the personal connection between the Holy Spirit and holy people.

Finally, Peter testifies that this loving God is patient and desires all people to come to repentance: "The Lord is not slow about His promise, as some count slowness, but is patient toward you, not wishing for any to perish but for all to come to repentance" (2 Pet 3:9). Christian orthodoxy does not assert that all people come to repentance or salvation. Nevertheless, Peter goes on record in accordance with the other New Testament writers about the loving, personal nature of God. God wills kindly things for people. Perhaps Peter bridges from the Old Testament prophet Ezekiel, who states that God takes no pleasure in the death or damnation of the wicked: "'Do I take any pleasure in the death of the wicked,' declares the Lord God, 'rather than that he would turn from his ways and live?' . . . 'I take no pleasure in the death of anyone who dies,' declares the Lord God.' 'Therefore, repent and live!'" (Ezek 18:23, 32)

At times one may hear the assessment that God as presented in the Old Testament is more severe than in the New Testament. A straightforward reading of the Bible indicates that God's nature does not change over time. Muslim readers can simply read through both testaments and make their own conclusions. In neither testament does the Almighty overlook sin. He is a holy God. Ultimately, He will not save those who reject the gift of salvation offered in Christ. He will assign those disbelievers to hell.

CONCLUSION

In this chapter, we have examined the contributions of the majority of New Testament writers regarding the loving, personal nature of God. Of the Great Eight, all were quoted except for Mark and Jude. These New Testament writings, which built upon several Old Testament texts, show remarkable unity on several points. First, the eternal God communicates directly with humans. Second, God is personal; He relates to people personally. Third, God is loving beyond comparison. The Great Eight Witnesses seem even to struggle to put God's loving nature into comprehensible words. Even now, I am still trying to fully fathom the depth of God's unconditional love.

As a young man who was born and raised Muslim, I read through the Bible at the age of nineteen (which is the magic number in Islam[4]). Though this experience occurred nearly forty years ago, I still recall some of my initial impressions. While many of the figures were well known to me as a Muslim, I initially was startled at how readily God spoke to people. As Muslims, we believed that Allah was merciful, which Christians also believe. Yet, the Bible presents a distinctly different portrayal regarding the personal and loving nature and character of God.

4. See Q74:30.

Chapter 7

Belief in the Divinity of Jesus

THE INQUIRY INTO WHEN, where, and how the early Christians may have gone astray continues with the examination of the specific beliefs held by Christians which are un-Islamic. The divinity of Jesus is the second Christian doctrine under consideration. The Qur'an specifically states, as was quoted above in Q5:72 and 5:116, that Jesus was neither divine nor did he ever claim to be divine in nature. Sura Ikhlas (112), verse 3, is well known to Muslims: *Lam yulid wa lam yulad* . . . "He has never had offspring, nor was He born." Clearly the doctrine of the divinity of Christ is un-Islamic and anti-qur'anic. If the Qur'an be true, then this must necessarily be a point at which Christians went astray.

It should be emphasized at the outset of this chapter that Christianity is a monotheistic religion. Christians have always believed and testified that there is only one God. The discussion of the divinity of Jesus, and later the Trinity, should be framed in this monotheistic context.

That Jesus' disciples came to believe in the divinity of Christ remains remarkable. Those disciples lived with Christ for three years. They walked with Him and ate with Him. Furthermore, these were Jewish men (and Jewish women were also part of the wider Jesus movement) who had been taught a clear demarcation exists between the Creator and created beings. The first two of the Ten Commandments warn against idolatry and idol-making. These Jewish disciples were not like gentiles for whom gods, goddesses, humans, and animals intersected and intermixed.

Incredibly, these followers of Jesus would go to the ends of the earth to preach that Jesus was the unique God-Man, sealing their testimony in their own blood in many cases. That Jesus' own half-brothers, who grew up in the same home as Him, and saw Him grow into the occupation of a carpenter, would later lead a church which proclaimed Jesus' divinity, likewise seems remarkable. Muslims may consider all of this, including the belief that Jesus was divine, to be astounding. Could it be a point in which Christians were somehow led astray?

Muslims commonly ask to see three words emanating from Jesus' mouth, "I am God." Since the Bible does not use this precise phrase, some Muslims conclude that Jesus never explicitly declared His divinity. They conclude, rather, that the divinity of Jesus was a later invention of straying Christians.[1]

It is possible to research the claims of Jesus regarding His own divinity. Chapter 3 demonstrated the relationships of Jesus to the Great Eight New Testament writers: Matthew, Mark, Luke, John, Paul, James, Peter, and Jude. Three of the Great Eight were from among His original twelve disciples, two were His half-brothers, one was a historical researcher who interviewed eyewitnesses at that time, one was a previous persecutor of Christians, and the last was a young man from a leading early Christian family. As a group, the Great Eight Witnesses were closely connected to Jesus. His disciples Peter and John knew Him as well as any living person.

If only one or two of the Great Eight reported Jesus' claims of divinity, then it might be possible to contend that the doctrine of Jesus' divinity was never intended by Jesus Himself. In that case, Christians would be guilty of straying. On the other hand, if the

---

1. By comparison, the Qur'an does not explicitly use the term *Tawhid*, though it can be argued that is the main theme of the Qur'an. Likewise, the Shahada is not explicitly found verbatim in the Qur'an, though it is the foundation of Islam.

Great Eight collectively corroborate the divinity of Jesus, then this doctrine would not likely be either a hijacker's imposition or a deceiver's invention.

Many Christian apologists over the centuries have written commentaries on the divinity of Jesus. Many Muslim polemicists over the centuries have written to deny the divinity of Jesus. This research seeks not to replicate that mountain of material and should not therefore be considered an exhaustive treatment of the subject. (As in other points, Muslim scholars and thinkers are invited to conduct their own independent research.) Rather, this inquiry specifically deals with answering when, where, or how Christians may have gone astray. In terms of this question, evidence exists regarding:

A. The views of Jesus' enemies and disbelievers regarding His divinity

B. Jesus' statements about His own divinity

C. Other statements about Jesus' divinity made by the Great Eight

These types of evidence will be pointed out where they occur. The flow of this chapter will continue the pattern of reviewing the writings of the Great Eight New Testament authors. What follows is a partial treatment of New Testament writings on the divinity of Jesus. I have not presented all the occurrences which I have cataloged in my own fresh rereading of the New Testament as I prepared to write this book.

Matthew: At the time the Holy Spirit conceived Jesus within the Virgin Mary, her fiancé Joseph naturally experienced concern and trepidation. He considered breaking off the engagement, since the relationship appeared scandalous. However, an angel appeared to him in a dream, saying:

> Joseph, son of David, do not be afraid to take Mary as your wife; for the Child who has been conceived in her is of the Holy Spirit. 21 She will give birth to a Son; and you shall name Him Jesus, for He will save His people from their sins." 22 Now all this took place so that what was spoken by the Lord through the prophet would be fulfilled: 23 "Behold, the virgin will conceive and give

> birth to a Son, and they shall name Him Immanuel,"
> which translated means, "God with us." (Matt 1:20–23)

Chapter 9 will consider the importance of Jesus' saving name, as described in verse 21 above.

Furthermore, Christians and Muslims agree regarding the virgin birth of Christ. Jesus was conceived and born without human sexual activity. The Holy Spirit of God was able to simply make the conception of Jesus happen without the normal procreative process by which humans come into the world.

The New Testament writers had in their possession the Old Testament. No doubt they studied it extensively. Matthew 1:23 provides a key early New Testament text about the divinity of Jesus. Here Matthew quotes from the prophet Isaiah (7:14), who prophesied six centuries earlier that God would provide a spectacular sign of a virgin conceiving, whose child would be called "Immanuel." The Arabic equivalent is *Allah maʾana,* "God is with us."

Clearly, a different meaning emanates from this passage other than simply the feeling of God being with us when things are going well in life. Those are times we may feel that God is with us, or His mercy is upon us. The context here is that a spectacular sign would occur: a virgin giving birth to a child named Immanuel.

Isaiah also describes in his book of prophecy (9:6), that the special messianic figure, the Christ, would also be "Mighty God:" "For a Child will be born to us, a Son will be given to us; And the government will rest on His shoulders; And His name will be called Wonderful Counselor, Mighty God, Eternal Father, Prince of Peace." As such, Jesus was the human child *born*, and the Son of God *given*—the Mighty God.

Soon after Jesus was born, wise men came from the East. They followed a star that led them to Bethlehem where Jesus had been born. Matthew narrates: "And after they came into the house, they saw the Child with His mother Mary; and they fell down and worshiped Him. Then they opened their treasures and presented to Him gifts of gold, frankincense, and myrrh" (Matt 2:11). Though Jesus was too young to receive or acclaim this worship, it marks the first of many instances in which people worshipped Jesus as Lord.

Another example of people worshipping Jesus occurred on one of several occasions where Jesus was on a boat with His disciples on the Sea of Galilee. On this occasion, Jesus bade Peter to walk upon the water, though waves were raging. Matthew narrates: "When they got into the boat, the wind stopped. And those who were in the boat worshiped Him, saying, 'You are truly God's Son!'" (Matt 14:32–33). In no case did Jesus prevent people from worshipping Him. In other cases where people erroneously prostrated themselves before men or angels, the men or angels rebuked them and told them to stand up.[2]

In Matt 8, the Gospel writer narrates the confrontation of Jesus and the Gerasene Demoniac, from whom Jesus cast a legion of demons into nearby pigs. When Jesus came into the presence of the demons, they reacted as follows: "And they cried out, saying, 'What business do You have with us, Son of God? Have You come here to torment us before the time?'" (Matt 8:29).[3] These demons knew they would later be condemned at the judgment day. They recognized Jesus as the Son of God and Divine Judge. This event constitutes oppositional acknowledgment of the divinity of Jesus.

Tension builds throughout the Gospels, particularly in the third year of Jesus' public ministry, as the Jewish religious leaders became committed to rejecting Jesus. They ultimately killed Him. During one such tense interaction, Jesus showed from the Old Testament that David referred to the Messiah (Greek, *Christos*) as "Lord," even though the Messiah would be a descendant of David. Matthew 22:41–46 reads:

> Now while the Pharisees were gathered together, Jesus asked them a question: 42 "What do you think about the Christ? Whose son is He?" They said to Him, "The son of David." 43 He said to them, "Then how does David in the Spirit call Him 'Lord,' saying,
> 44 'The Lord said to my Lord, "Sit at My right hand, Until I put Your enemies under Your feet"'?

2. See Acts 10: 25–26; Rev 22:8–9.

3. For parallel references, see Mark 5:7; Luke 8:28.

45 Therefore, if David calls Him 'Lord,' how is He his son?" 46 No one was able to offer Him a word in answer, nor did anyone dare from that day on to ask Him any more questions.

Jesus demonstrates that He is not only the son of David, but also the Lord of David. His quotation from David's psalm "The Lord said to my Lord" (Ps 110:1), also indicates a plurality in the Godhead. Communication exists within the Godhead, as illustrated here. This inquiry will revisit this topic in the next chapter on the Triune God.

Mark: The second Gospel provides perhaps the clearest statement by Jesus regarding His own divinity. Muslim students of theology will be able to determine the intent of Jesus in the testimony of the Healing of the Paralytic. The full passage of Mark 2:1–12 is given for context, with key portions emphasized:

When Jesus came back to Capernaum a few days later, it was heard that He was at home. 2 And many were gathered together, so that there was no longer space, not even near the door; and He was speaking the word to them. 3 And some people came, bringing to Him a man who was paralyzed, carried by four men. 4 And when they were unable to get to Him because of the crowd, they removed the roof above Him; and after digging an opening, they let down the pallet on which the paralyzed man was lying. 5 And Jesus, seeing their faith, said to the paralyzed man, "Son, your sins are forgiven." 6 But some of the scribes were sitting there and thinking it over in their hearts, 7 "Why does this man speak that way? He is blaspheming! *Who can forgive sins except God alone?*" 8 Immediately Jesus, aware in His spirit that they were thinking that way within themselves, said to them, "Why are you thinking about these things in your hearts? 9 Which is easier, to say to the paralyzed man, 'Your sins are forgiven'; or to say, 'Get up, and pick up your pallet and walk'? 10 *But so that you may know that the Son of Man has authority on earth to forgive sins"*— He said to the paralyzed man, 11 "I say to you, get up, pick up your pallet, and go home." 12 And he got up and immediately picked up the pallet and went out in the sight of everyone, so that they were all amazed and were glorifying God, saying, "We have never seen anything like this!"

About eight years ago I was giving a series of lectures at an American university in Texas. Several Muslim students from Saudi Arabia attended. One asked the question: "Where in the Bible does Jesus say, 'I am God?'" I responded by reading this passage. I also gave them an Arabic Bible. I challenged them to study the passage. I offered them the microphone at the next night's lecture to report whether Jesus was claiming divinity in the passage. I emphasized that the question was not whether *they believed* Jesus to be divine, but whether Jesus *was claiming* to be divine. However, they did not return the next evening or subsequent evenings.

This passage in Mark 2 demonstrates the angst felt among many when Jesus claimed the power to forgive sins. An Old Testament precedent existed for mortals to heal the sick, but God alone retained the right to forgive and absolve people of their sins. Jesus knew this, of course. Thus, He provoked the situation by declaring someone's sins to be forgiven. If He did not intend to claim divinity, He would have immediately backtracked in the narration above. Yet, He states emphatically, "so that you may know that the Son of Man has authority on earth to forgive sins" (v. 10). It is difficult to explain this situation other than that Jesus was intentionally and clearly claiming divinity.

The New Testament narrates the growing belief on the part of Jesus' disciples that He was divine. He was both Son of Man and Son of God, in that He was both fully human and fully divine. On an occasion in which Jesus immediately stopped the raging waves on the Sea of Galilee, it began to dawn on the disciples that this was no ordinary prophet or rabbi: "They became very much afraid and said to one another, "Who then is this, that even the wind and the sea obey Him?" (Mark 4:41). It must have been both an awesome and fearsome experience for the disciples as the light dawned in their minds and hearts that their Master was no mere mortal.

John: The strongest New Testament support for the divinity of Jesus is provided not by Paul, but by John. John wrote last among the New Testament writers and could have corrected any incorrect elevation of a mortal Jesus, had he perceived such correction to be warranted. To the contrary, John confirms what the other Gospel writers wrote about Jesus' divinity. He provides unique narration to a number of events and dialogs which affirm this orthodox Christian doctrine.

John begins his Gospel not with the birth of the baby Jesus, but with a description of the pre-existent and eternal Son of God. He describes Jesus as the Word[4] which "became flesh and dwelt among us" (John 1:14). This Word (Greek, *Logos*), Jesus, is divine and the Creator of all things: "In the beginning was the Word, and the Word was with God, and the Word was God. 2 He was in the beginning with God. 3 All things came into being through Him, and apart from Him nothing came into being that has come into being" (John 1:1–3).

The Muslim reader can make his or her own assessment about Jesus as described here in John's Gospel. Those looking for the three words from Jesus, "I am God," may find the phrase "And the Word was God" similar enough. This passage obviously has implications for plurality in the Godhead, as will be explored in the next chapter.

Muslims will remember the tension in the Islamic narrative between the people of Mecca who opposed Muhammad and those who believed him. A similar tension occurs in the four Gospels. John highlights the tension between those who accepted Jesus as Messiah and Lord, and those who rejected Him. Several of these interactions indicate that those who disbelieved in Jesus knew He claimed divinity. In one case, Jesus healed a man on the sabbath, which was considered a violation of the sabbath. Jesus continually explained His relationship to the Heavenly Father:

4. The Qur'an describes Jesus as the Word of Allah, *kalimatuhu*, in Q4:171. However, as understood by Muslims, this is not a divine Logos, but a prophet who spoke the words of Allah, as did all other prophets.

For this reason the Jews were persecuting Jesus, because He was doing these things on the Sabbath. 17 But He answered them, "My Father is working until now, and I Myself am working." 18 For this reason therefore the Jews were seeking all the more to kill Him, because He not only was breaking the Sabbath, but also was calling God His own Father, making Himself equal with God. (John 5:16–18)

The disbelievers commonly derided Jesus as being inferior to Moses as well as to Abraham. During one such interchange, Jesus used the expression "I am" to indicate He pre-dated Abraham. He claimed for Himself to be the Eternal One. His opponents picked up stones to kill Him for blasphemy, for equating Himself with God. This passage begins with Jesus speaking to His opponents:

Your father Abraham rejoiced to see My day, and he saw it and was glad." 57 So the Jews said to Him, "You are not yet fifty years old, and have You seen Abraham?" 58 Jesus said to them, "Truly, truly, I say to you, before Abraham was born, I am." 59 Therefore they picked up stones to throw at Him, but Jesus hid Himself and went out of the temple. (John 8:56–59)

In John 10 a similar interchange occurs, beginning with Jesus speaking:

"My sheep hear My voice, and I know them and they follow Me; 28 and I give eternal life to them, and they will never perish; and no one will snatch them out of My hand. 29 My Father, who has given them to Me, is greater than all; and no one is able to snatch them out of the Father's hand. 30 I and the Father are one."
31 The Jews picked up stones again to stone Him. 32 Jesus answered them, "I showed you many good works from the Father; for which of them are you stoning Me?" 33 The Jews answered Him, "For a good work we do not stone You, but for blasphemy; and because You, being a man, make Yourself out to be God." (John 10:27–33)

Several points can be observed. First, Jesus gives eternal life (v. 28) which is a divine prerogative. Second, the believers are figuratively in the safe hands of *both* the Father and the Son (vv. 28–29). Third, Jesus states that He and the Father are one (v. 30). Finally, from this incident, His opponents pick up stones again to stone Him. They claim He has blasphemed, "You, being a man, make Yourself out to be God" (v. 33).

Furthermore, during Jesus' final hours before going to the cross, He appeared before the Roman governor Pontius Pilate. Pilate did not want to execute Jesus, but the Jewish leaders enlisted Roman support because they did not want to become ceremonially unclean by executing a person on the Passover holiday. They explained to Pilate that they were obligated by the Law of Moses to kill Jesus for blasphemy: "The Jews answered him, We have a law, and by that law He ought to die because He made Himself out to be the Son of God'" (John 19:7).[5] They charged Jesus with blasphemy because of His claim to divinity.

Throughout this narrative, Jesus' Sonship has nothing to do with God having a consort or sexual relations with Mary. All the observers understood that Jesus was claiming divinity. As punishment for this, they believed He deserved to die.

Several incidents occur in John's Gospel in which Jesus received worship. In chapter 9, He healed a man born blind. The man returned to worship Jesus (John 9:38). Later, after Jesus' resurrection, He appeared to His disciples. Thomas, who was absent for Jesus' first post-Resurrection appearance, was skeptical. However, Jesus later appeared to the disciples again. He specifically asked Thomas to touch the wounds He suffered on the cross. Thomas did so, and then became a believer in Christ's divinity: "Thomas answered and said to Him, 'My Lord and my God!' 29 Jesus said to him, 'Because you have seen Me, have you believed? Blessed are they who did not see, and yet believed'"

---

5. Apparently the "law" referred to is Lev 24:16: "Moreover, the one who blasphemes the name of the Lord shall surely be put to death; all the congregation shall certainly stone him. The alien as well as the native, when he blasphemes the Name, shall be put to death."

(John 20:28–29). Jesus did not correct Thomas for exclaiming Him as Lord and God.

Muslim readers also know that the qur'anic Jesus worked miracles, "by Allah's will."[6] Thus, a miracle-working Jesus does not contradict the qur'anic narrative. Both the Bible and Qur'an report that Jesus could raise the dead. However, when Jesus rose from the dead in the Gospel narratives, no one prayed for Him to revive. He rose by the divine resurrection power within Himself. The book of Hebrews describes this as the "power of an indestructible life" (Heb 7:16).

Luke: This inquiry has noted some parallel passages between Matthew, Mark, and Luke. Not all have been listed in the footnotes, since those references can easily be found online by any concerned researcher. Luke provides a unique account of some of the events surrounding Jesus' birth. At the time Jesus was born, an angel of the Lord appeared to shepherds in Bethlehem, telling them: "Today in the city of David there has been born for you a Savior, who is Christ the Lord" (Luke 2:11). Even at Jesus' birth, He received the title "Lord," which is the Greek word *Kurios*.

Muslims reserve the title "Lord" for God, though in various languages the term "lord" does not necessarily mean divinity. The English language uses such a term to describe "feudal lords" or "landlords," as well as the Lord of Heaven and Earth. The Arabic *Rabb* as in Fatiha, ayah 2, *Rabb al-'Alameen*, means The Lord of the Worlds. The Hebrew cognate of the Arabic *Rabb* is used for rabbi, which can also describe a human teacher.

I present these linguistic explanations for several reasons. First, the New Testament writers and the disciples of Jesus refer commonly to Jesus as Lord (*Kurios*). Luke narrates a seemingly improbable scenario in which the carpenter Jesus tells the fisherman Peter where he can catch fish. Peter is dismayed by this, since they have fished all night and caught nothing. When he obeys Jesus and lets down his nets where Jesus has indicated, they catch such "a great quantity of fish" that it is tearing their nets. Obviously, Jesus was presenting a miracle to His new disciple Peter. Luke narrates,

6. See, for example, Q3:49.

"When Simon Peter saw this, he fell down at Jesus' knees, saying, "Go away from me, *Lord*, for I am a sinful man!" (Luke 5:8, emphasis added). The context here of falling at Jesus' feet, acknowledging the miracle, as well as his own sinfulness, coupled with the use of "Lord," indicates Peter had begun to see Jesus as someone beyond a mere human rabbi.

Second, the orthodox Christian doctrine of the divinity of Christ does not rest solely on Jesus being referred to as *Kurios*, since this term is far from the sole descriptor of divinity. I have provided several examples, though dozens more occur in the New Testament. Luke narrates Peter describing Jesus as *Kurios* in Acts 2:36. Paul, then known as Saul, addresses Jesus as *Kurios* in Acts 22:8, 10. Third, other stronger evidence exists for Jesus' divinity, as we have seen, and as we will continue to see. In some cases, *Kurios* is paired with another descriptor of divinity for appositional emphasis.

Paul: In his epistles, Paul consistently affirms the divinity of Jesus. To the Romans, he states that Jesus "was declared the Son of God with power by the resurrection from the dead, according to the Spirit of holiness, Jesus Christ our Lord" (Rom 1:4). He instructs the Corinthian Church that affirming the Lordship of Christ is central to the faith: "Therefore I make known to you that no one speaking by the Spirit of God says, 'Jesus is accursed'; and no one can say, 'Jesus is Lord,' except by the Holy Spirit" (1 Cor 12:3). In the same way that affirming the divinity of Christ makes someone a non-Muslim, affirming the divinity of Christ is essential for meeting the Scriptural standard of being an authentic Christian.

To the Colossians, Paul wrote of Jesus, "For in Him all the fullness of Deity dwells in bodily form" (Col 2:9). When Paul wrote to his disciple Titus, he instructed him to be "looking for the blessed hope and the appearing of the glory of our great God and Savior, Christ Jesus" (Tit 2:13). From these passages, a picture emerges in which Paul believes in the full divinity of Jesus.

Perhaps Paul's most helpful contribution to Christology, as it pertains to Muslims understanding the God-Man phenomenon, appears in his letter to the Philippians. Paul ministered in Philippi in Acts 16, where he was beaten and jailed. In this epistle, Paul writes that Jesus existed as God, but "emptied" Himself (v. 7 below) of some of the qualities of divinity to take on human form and live among humans. The Greek word for emptying is *Kenosis*, which is part of orthodox Christology. Paul writes:

> Have this attitude in yourselves which was also in Christ Jesus, 6 who, although He existed in the form of God, did not regard equality with God a thing to be grasped, 7 but emptied Himself, taking the form of a bond-servant, and being made in the likeness of men. 8 Being found in appearance as a man, He humbled Himself by becoming obedient to the point of death, even death on a cross. 9 For this reason also, God highly exalted Him, and bestowed on Him the name which is above every name, 10 so that at the name of Jesus every knee will bow, of those who are in heaven and on earth and under the earth, 11 and that every tongue will confess that Jesus Christ is Lord, to the glory of God the Father. (Phil 2:5–11)

The *Kenosis* refers to a laying aside of some divine privileges. This helps the New Testament reader understand why Jesus could say He did not know when exactly He would return to earth. In John's Gospel, which strongly emphasizes the divinity of Jesus, Jesus states, "The Father is greater than I" (John 14:28). In that verse, Jesus specifically refers to His visit to earth and His forthcoming ascension to heaven.

Hebrews: The writer of Hebrews takes pains to show that Jesus the Son is different in nature than either angels or prophets. The epistle starts with a short prologue about Christ, which will also be considered in the next chapter on the Triune God. Hebrews 1 then contrasts Jesus with angels by using Old Testament quotations, which would naturally be very relevant to a Jewish audience: "Of the angels He says, 'Who makes His angels winds, And His ministers a flame of fire.' But of the Son He says, 'Your throne, O God, is forever and ever'" (Heb 1:7–8). The former quote regarding angels is from Ps 104:4, the latter quote regarding the Son is from Ps 45:6. The key transition term "but" indicates that the Son has a completely different nature than that of angels.

In Heb 3, the author makes clear to the readers that Jesus possesses a different nature than even Moses, who was considered the greatest prophet among the Jewish nation. The author likens Moses to the servant in a household, while Christ is presented as the son and heir of the house. The son and heir have the same nature as the father who is the householder.

> Therefore, holy brethren, partakers of a heavenly calling, consider Jesus, the Apostle and High Priest of our confession; 2 He was faithful to Him who appointed Him, as Moses also was in all His house. 3 For He has been counted worthy of more glory than Moses, by just so much as the builder of the house has more honor than the house. 4 For every house is built by someone, but the builder of all things is God. 5 Now Moses was faithful in all His house as a servant, for a testimony of those things which were to be spoken later; 6 but Christ was faithful as a Son over His house—whose house we are, if we hold fast our confidence and the boast of our hope firm until the end. (Heb 3:1–6)

Both Moses and Jesus were faithful in fulfilling their respective callings, yet Jesus the Son of God was of a different nature than Moses the servant of God. Jesus had a different nature than the angels who serve God. He has a divine nature.

James: James, in his call to vital Christian living, describes his half-brother Jesus as "our glorious Lord Jesus Christ" (Jas 2:1). This represents another amplified use of *Kurios* in relation to Jesus. The superlative "glorious Lord" is not a phrase that one would ever use of a prophet or human rabbi.

Peter: Peter, the close disciple of Christ, opens his second epistle with a strong statement regarding the divinity of Jesus: "Simon Peter, a bond-servant and apostle of Jesus Christ, To those who have received a faith of the same kind as ours, by the righteousness of our God and Savior, Jesus Christ: Grace and peace be multiplied to you in the knowledge of God and of Jesus our Lord"

(2 Pet 1:1–2). In this introduction, Peter refers to Jesus Christ as God, Savior, and Lord. If Peter merely considered himself the disciple of a human rabbi, he would have used respectful terms regarding Jesus, but he would not have used any of these terms. As the student of a rabbi, he would have aspired to grow into the same type of rabbi himself. Yet, Peter states that he is the "bond-servant" of Christ.

CONCLUSION

While the divinity of Jesus may present a stumbling block for Muslims—we were all taught that the very concept was a blasphemy—the Great Eight New Testament writers overwhelmingly attest that this is their belief. Matthew, John, and Peter walked with Jesus for all of Christ's public ministry. Had Jesus only claimed to be a mortal prophet or human rabbi, they would have vehemently contested anyone who claimed Jesus was divine. Yet, they all acclaim Christ as the Divine Son of God, with John—the final New Testament writer—issuing perhaps the strongest call of the Great Eight.

Of the doctrines presented in this study which can be considered anti-Islamic, the divinity of Christ receives as much New Testament support as any other. This chapter comprises the longest of the book, though I omitted a number of references—simply for the sake of space and avoiding redundance—that could also have been presented regarding the divinity of Christ. All this data can be considered by open-minded Muslim scholars and thinkers. My goal is to present evidence. Everyone should prepare to make final decisions for himself or herself.

Chapter 8

Belief in the Triune God

I WAS BORN AND raised Muslim. I have now been a Christian for forty years. I have talked with Muslims, Christians, Christian-background Muslims, and Muslim-background Christians. I acknowledge that the Christian doctrine of the Triune God, also known as the Holy Trinity, is a difficult one for Muslims to understand and embrace. Perhaps it is as challenging as the doctrine of the divinity of Christ addressed in the previous chapter. It should be emphasized at the beginning of this chapter that Christians believe in One God and have always believed in One God.

I believe five main reasons exist for the challenge confronting those of us born and raised as Muslims. First, we have been taught about *Tawhid* and against Trinity from childhood. This creates an inestimable impact upon the mind and the soul.

Second, the presence of the Triune God as Holy Trinity is meant to be experienced *before and during* the process of understanding the doctrine. The experiential process for Christian believers tends to proceed as follows: The Holy Spirit convinces people of their sinfulness and need for a Savior. Jesus Christ, the Divine Eternal Son of God, presents Himself as that Savior. The believer in Jesus, having been born again, becomes a child of the Heavenly Father. Those who have gone through this personal experience will be more likely to mentally grasp the biblical doctrine of the one Triune God, or Holy Trinity.

Third, embracing the Trinity makes a Muslim an apostate. This book has not focused on this reality. However, the fear of apostasy is the backdrop upon which life is painted for many Muslims. We have been taught that honorable people do not leave the final religion, the faith of our parents and grandparents. We must acknowledge this reality so that we can address it. Fear should not rule over us.

Fourth, Christians often define the Trinity as "one God in three Persons—Father, Son, and Holy Spirit." As a young Christian myself, I was confused by the expression "three persons." In this chapter, we will examine the meaning and usage of this terminology.

Fifth, based on the previous reasons, and especially the third one regarding the fear of apostasy, Muslims typically do not explore whether biblical doctrines such as the Triune God are actually true or false. This reality impacts the central question of when, where, and how Christians may have gone astray. The answer is simply assumed, but never explored. This chapter seeks to apply the research methodology regarding the Great Eight New Testament writers to the plausibility of the Trinity.

BUILDING A NEW TESTAMENT DOCTRINE

Christian theology comes from the Bible. The doctrine of the Trinity is hinted at even in the Old Testament. It comes into full picture in the New Testament. What do those texts teach? Indeed, Christians for 2,000 years have been unequivocal in their belief that the One God exists eternally as Father, Son, and Holy Spirit.[1]

1. Chapter 10 considers areas where Christians have gone astray. One non-biblical tradition which crept in around the time of the advent of Islam was the elevation of the Virgin Mary. Catholics began to address prayer and intercession to Mary. It may be for this reason that the Qur'an assumes the Trinity to be the Father, the Mother, and the Son, as per Q5:116: And on Judgment Day Allah will say, "O Jesus, son of Mary! Did you ever ask the people to worship you and your mother as gods besides Allah?" However, the orthodox Christian

PART III

The previous chapter provided significant evidence for the divinity of Christ. That doctrine becomes one pillar, or *rukn*, in building out the teaching of the Holy Trinity. This chapter will consider data regarding the divinity of the Heavenly Father as well as the divinity of the Holy Spirit, before presenting the total picture regarding the One Triune God.

OLD TESTAMENT REFERENCES TO THE TRINITY

An old joke exists—perhaps it really happened—in which a Christian Sunday School teacher asked young children: "Why does God seem harsher in the Old Testament, but more loving in the New Testament?" A young child answered, "Because in the New Testament, God became a Christian!"

In fact, the premise of the teacher's question was wrong. God does not change His nature over the course of the Bible. Everything revealed in the New Testament is presented in the Old Testament. So it is with the doctrine of the Trinity. Even now, a full treatment of Old Testament references regarding plurality within the Godhead would dwarf the current size of this book. This research will simply provide a sketch of the evidence for Muslim scholars and thinkers to analyze. All are welcome to read through the entire Bible to make their own conclusions.

The opening chapter of the Bible presents the teaching of plurality within the Godhead, as well as the Trinitarian nature of God. Chapter 6 above quoted from Gen 1:26: "Then God said, 'Let Us make man in Our image, according to Our likeness.'" This verse indicates plurality evident within the Godhead such that one God is able to communicate within Himself. So, not only must God exhibit some plurality within His unity, but He is able to communicate within Himself in a personal manner.

The very first verses of Genesis narrate a Trinitarian event: "In the beginning God created the heavens and the earth. 2 The

---

position has never included Mary in the Trinity.

earth was formless and void, and darkness was over the surface of the deep, and the Spirit of God was moving over the surface of the waters. 3 Then God said, 'Let there be light'; and there was light" (Gen 1:1–3).

In this passage, God, who always existed, is portrayed as Creator. God is present, the Spirit of God is present, and the Word of God is also present. This account provides the first biblical presentation of the Triune God.

According to John 1:3, which was reviewed in the last chapter, the Son of God, whom John calls the Word or *Logos*, is the Creator of all things. Genesis 1:1 states that God created the heavens and the earth. The prophet Job, known in Arabic as *Ayub*, went through great sufferings which his friends sought to explain. Job quotes his friend Elihu who states that the Spirit of God is the Creator: "The Spirit of God has made me, And the breath of the Almighty gives me life" (Job 33:4).

One mental challenge confronting Muslims in their consideration of the One Triune God is that no human situation portrays absolutely perfect unity. No team or company features perfect unity. No marital couple can boast perfect unity. However, the Holy Trinity portrays perfect unity. This explains why the Bible references Father, Son, and Holy Spirit as Creator equally and simultaneously.

Due to the emphasis of this research upon the New Testament, we will transition to that source. Abundant scriptural evidence exists in the Old Testament for appearances of Christ, known as theophanies, or Christophanies.[2] Muslims who want to investigate Old Testament Christophanies will find a host of internet sources on the subject. Specifically, the Old Testament chronicles many appearances of an "angel of the Lord" of whom divine language descriptors are used. Abraham meets this figure in Gen 18, for example.

The previous chapter on the divinity of Christ quoted Isaiah's prophecies, 7:14 and 9:6, which gives an early testimony to the Fatherhood of God. Isaiah also paints a picture of the Holy Trinity

2. See Simnowitz, "Son of God."

in a messianic passage of Isa 48:12–16. The key verse is 16, but the passage gives the full context of God speaking, who calls himself the Creator, as well as the First and the Last:

> "Listen to Me, O Jacob, even Israel whom I called;
> I am He, I am the first, I am also the last.
> 13 "Surely My hand founded the earth,
> And My right hand spread out the heavens;
> When I call to them, they stand together.
> 14 "Assemble, all of you, and listen!
> Who among them has declared these things?
> The Lord loves him; he will carry out His good pleasure
> on Babylon,
> And His arm will be against the Chaldeans.
> 15 "I, even I, have spoken; indeed I have called him,
> I have brought him, and He will make his ways successful.
> 16 "Come near to Me, listen to this:
> From the first I have not spoken in secret,
> From the time it took place, I was there.
> And now the Lord God has sent Me, and His Spirit."

In this passage, God says that the Lord God has sent Him, and His Spirit. Three references to deity occur simultaneously. The verse prophesies the sending forth of the Son.

THE GREAT EIGHT AND THE ONE TRIUNE GOD

The New Testament writers provide material about the Trinity which can be divided into two basic categories:

A. Narration of Trinitarian Manifestations and Events

B. Teachings that Establish the Trinitarian Nature of God

Matthew: Matthew is the first of the three Synoptic Gospel writers who record the baptism of Jesus.[3] This description falls into the first category—the narration of a Trinitarian event.

---

3. See also Mark 1:9–11; Luke 3:22.

> 13 Then Jesus arrived from Galilee at the Jordan coming to John, to be baptized by him. 14 But John tried to prevent Him, saying, "I have need to be baptized by You, and do You come to me?" 15 But Jesus answering said to him, "Permit it at this time; for in this way it is fitting for us to fulfill all righteousness." Then he permitted Him. 16 After being baptized, Jesus came up immediately from the water; and behold, the heavens were opened, and he saw the Spirit of God descending as a dove and lighting on Him, 17 and behold, a voice out of the heavens said, "This is My beloved Son, in whom I am well-pleased." (Matt 3:13–17)

Several points of observation beckon the reader. First, the Spirit of God descended upon Christ at His baptism.[4] Second, a voice came from heaven which recognizes the beloved Son of God. The voice must be that of the Heavenly Father, though the Gospel writers do not provide a name to that voice. In the previous chapter, the apostle John highlighted the relationship between the Father and the Son. Thus, the Father, Son, and Spirit manifest together at this Trinitarian event.

Third, Muslims have often asked who would run the universe in the case of God visiting the earth in flesh, as Christians believe. Ibn Qayyim al Jawziyya famously poses this same question in his medieval poetic challenge, "O Christ Worshippers!"[5] The biblical narration here provides a simple and ready answer. The Father remained in heaven during the time the Son came to the earth to fulfill His redemptive purpose.

Matthew also records the second type of Trinitarian narration—directly from the teaching of Jesus Himself. Prior to Jesus returning to heaven, He gave important instructions to His disciples in an address known as the "Great Commission." Matthew states:

> And Jesus came up and spoke to them, saying, "All authority has been given to Me in heaven and on earth. 19 Go therefore and make disciples of all the nations, baptizing

4. The Spirit's descent did not deify Jesus. He already existed as God at that time.

5. Jawziyyah, "O Christ-Worshippers!"

them in the name of the Father and the Son and the Holy
Spirit, 20 teaching them to observe all that I commanded
you; and lo, I am with you always, even to the end of the
age." (Matt 28:18–20)

The baptism of believers in Christ marks the entry passage
into the body of Christ. Jesus instructed His disciples to baptize
new disciples "in the name of the Father and the Son and the Holy
Spirit" (v. 19). Readers may note that Jesus did not say "in the
names of . . ." Neither did Jesus say, "in the name of the Father, and
in the name of the Son, and in the name of the Holy Spirit." Rather,
He identified the One God as named Father, Son, and Holy Spirit.
The Greek uses the singular word for "name" (*onoma*). Thus, the
first Gospel sets a strong basis for the orthodox Christian belief in
One Triune God.

Mark: The previous chapter discussed at length the support
of the Great Eight for the divinity of Jesus. This chapter investigates
New Testament evidence for the divinity of the Holy Spirit. Muslims often associate the Holy Spirit with Gabriel, based on Q2:97
and Q16:102. In these verses, Gabriel, and then the Holy Spirit, are
described as bringing down the revelation in truth. Islamic theology maintains that neither Gabriel nor the Holy Spirit is divine.
Therefore, this chapter will give ample attention to establishing the
Christian doctrine of the divinity of the Holy Spirit.

Both Islam and Christianity have a teaching regarding unpardonable sins. In Islam, according to Q4:116, *shirk* is the unforgivable sin. Jesus stated that the unforgivable sin is "blasphemy
against the Holy Spirit." The context of Jesus making this statement
was a contentious event in which religious scribes from Jerusalem accused Jesus of doing miracles by the power of Satan. Jesus
explained the ridiculousness of such a statement. He concluded
by saying: "Truly I say to you, all sins shall be forgiven the sons
of men, and whatever blasphemies they utter; but whoever blasphemes against the Holy Spirit never has forgiveness, but is guilty
of an eternal sin" (Mark 3:28–29).

Christians have long pondered exactly what Jesus meant by
this saying. The context describes the dramatic hardening of the

human heart which could attribute the miracles of Jesus to Satan. The key takeaway for this discussion involves the concept of blasphemy against the highest power, described here as the Holy Spirit.

John: The previous chapter depicted John's emphasis on the unity of the Father and the Son. John also records Jesus' teaching at the Last Supper, known at the Upper Room Discourse. This discourse, found in John 14–16, brings the Holy Spirit into the Johannine theological framework.

John captures the words of Jesus in several trinitarian statements. Jesus, who would soon ascend to heaven, wanted to instruct His disciples about the roles of the Father, Son, and Holy Spirit: "These things I have spoken to you while abiding with you. But the Helper, the Holy Spirit, whom the Father will send in My name, He will teach you all things, and bring to your remembrance all that I said to you" (John 14:25–26). The same Spirit, sent by the Father in Jesus' name, would assist the disciples in remembering the words of Christ. One byproduct of this assistance resulted in Matthew, John, and Peter writing portions of the New Testament.[6]

In John 15, Jesus makes a similar statement, indicating that both He and the Father are able to send the Spirit: "When the Helper comes, whom I will send to you from the Father, that is the Spirit of truth who proceeds from the Father, He will testify about Me, 27 and you will testify also, because you have been with Me from the beginning" (John 15:26–27). The combination of these two passages reinforces what Jesus said in John 10:30, "I and the Father are one."

One final passage from the Upper Room Discourse cements the interaction of Father, Son, and Spirit, particularly in assisting the disciples of Jesus:

> When He, the Spirit of truth, comes, He will guide you into
> all the truth; for He will not speak on His own initiative,
> but whatever He hears, He will speak; and He will disclose

---

6. Muslims frequently state that the Helper or Comforter spoken of here by Jesus is actually Muhammad. However, this Helper was to assist those specific disciples of Jesus. Muhammad, who appeared six centuries later, could not have fulfilled this role.

> to you what is to come. 14 He will glorify Me, for He will take of Mine and will disclose it to you. 15 All things that the Father has are Mine; therefore I said that He takes of Mine and will disclose it to you. (John 16:13–15)

John gives particular emphasis to the relationship of the Father and the Son. In the Upper Room Discourse, Jesus explains the roles and interaction of Father, Son, and Spirit—the One God whom Jesus' disciples will serve.

Luke: Luke describes a Trinitarian event regarding the conception of Jesus. Again, God the Holy Spirit plays a central role as the Divine Son would come to earth. When the Angel Gabriel visited Mary to announce she would give birth as a virgin to Jesus, she was rightly concerned: "Mary said to the angel, 'How can this be, since I am a virgin?' 35 The angel answered and said to her, 'The Holy Spirit will come upon you, and the power of the Most High will overshadow you; and for that reason the holy Child shall be called the Son of God'" (Luke 1:34–35).

The Son of God would be conceived by the Holy Spirit and through the power of the Most High. No human sexual activity accompanied the conception of Jesus. God is able to speak a creative word to bring something into existence, as He did with the creative word in Gen 1:3: "Let there be light!" In this case, He caused the conception of a baby in the womb of Mary by the miraculous action of the Holy Spirit.

Luke also provides an unmistakable reference to the divinity of the Holy Spirit in the Acts of the Apostles. In Acts 5, a scandal rocked the early church. Many believers were making charitable offerings to help the growing movement. A husband and wife, Ananias and Sapphira, lied about their gift of a land sale. Peter, who was leading the church at that time, confronted them. In doing so, Peter uses language which clearly equates the Holy Spirit with God:

> Peter said, "Ananias, why has Satan filled your heart to *lie to the Holy Spirit* and to keep back some of the price of the land? 4 While it remained unsold, did it not remain your own? And after it was sold, was it not under your

control? Why is it that you have conceived this deed in your heart? You have not *lied to men but to God.*" (Acts 5:3–4, emphasis added)

Ananias lied to the Holy Spirit. In the next breath, Peter states that Ananias lied to God.

Luke utilizes a similar mechanism in comparing Jesus to the Holy Spirit. The occasion is the second missionary journey, conducted by Paul, Silas, and Timothy. Luke narrates: "They passed through the Phrygian and Galatian region, having been forbidden by the Holy Spirit to speak the word in Asia; 7 and after they came to Mysia, they were trying to go into Bithynia, and the Spirit of Jesus did not permit them" (Acts 16:6–7). Acts presents Jesus and the Holy Spirit in perfect, harmonious unity.

Paul: Paul provides many writings which affirm the trinitarian nature of God. He upholds the divinity of the Father, Son, and Holy Spirit, sometimes through coupling terminology. He exhorts the Corinthians: "You were justified in the name of the Lord Jesus Christ and in the Spirit of our God" (1 Cor 6:11). He concludes the second epistle to the Corinthians with a trinitarian benediction: "The grace of the Lord Jesus Christ, and the love of God, and the fellowship of the Holy Spirit, be with you all" (2 Cor 13:14).

Paul wrote several written prayers on behalf of the church at Ephesus. One such prayer includes a trinitarian supplication:

> For this reason I bow my knees before the Father, 15 from whom every family in heaven and on earth derives its name, 16 that He would grant you, according to the riches of His glory, to be strengthened with power through His Spirit in the inner man, 17 so that Christ may dwell in your hearts through faith. (Eph 3:14–17)

Paul likewise links Christ and the Spirit of God, who is the Holy Spirit, when he writes to the early church at Rome: "However, you are not in the flesh but in the Spirit, if indeed the Spirit of God dwells in you. But if anyone does not have the Spirit of Christ, he does not belong to Him" (Rom 8:9).

Thus, Paul affirms the writings of his brethren regarding the Holy Trinity. By no means does Paul emerge as the most prolific New Testament writer on the Trinity. Had Paul been trying to hijack Christianity by interposing a novel doctrine such as the Trinity, then we would have expected a unique angle from Paul and his proliferation of material on the subject. Rather, Paul merely contributes to and corroborates the growing New Testament theology on the One Triune God.

Peter: In Peter's first epistle, this disciple of Jesus Christ writes the following salutation:

> Peter, an apostle of Jesus Christ, to those who reside as aliens, scattered throughout Pontus, Galatia, Cappadocia, Asia, and Bithynia, who are chosen 2 according to the foreknowledge of God the Father, by the sanctifying work of the Spirit, to obey Jesus Christ and be sprinkled with His blood: May grace and peace be yours in the fullest measure. (1 Pet 1:1–2)

Peter describes himself as an apostle of Jesus Christ—who is to be obeyed. This language demonstrates the Lordship of Christ. God the Father foreknew who would come to faith. These believers would be sanctified by the Holy Spirit. Peter the monotheist uses trinitarian language in reference to the relationship of believers to God.

Furthermore, in a passage quoted earlier, Peter states that the Holy Spirit is the inspirer of Scripture. "Know this first of all, that no prophecy of Scripture is a matter of one's own interpretation, 21 for no prophecy was ever made by an act of human will, but men moved by the Holy Spirit spoke from God" (2 Pet 1:20–21). Since the Holy Spirit is the same agent inspiring all the biblical writers, then it is not surprising that their message is unified. For 1,400 years, these inspired writers pointed to the Lord Jesus Christ.

Jude: The half-brother of Christ wrote a short warning epistle against false prophets. In the transition to his conclusion, Jude writes: "But you, beloved, building yourselves up on your most holy faith, praying in the Holy Spirit, 21 keep yourselves in the love of God, waiting anxiously for the mercy of our Lord Jesus Christ to eternal life" (vv. 20–21). Here Jude offers one of many references to Christ as *Kurios*. He also states that the holy faith includes praying in the Holy Spirit and keeping oneself in the love of God. The trajectory of this teaching points to plurality in the Godhead.

Hebrews: The writer of Hebrews dedicates the prologue of this letter to the topic of Christology. Jesus, the Creator, is described as the "radiance of the glory of God" and "the exact representation of His nature":

> God, after He spoke long ago to the fathers in the prophets in many portions and in many ways, 2 in these last days has spoken to us in His Son, whom He appointed heir of all things, through whom also He made the world. 3 And He is the radiance of His glory and the exact representation of His nature. (Heb 1:1–3a)

Challenges abound in describing the infinite and matchless Creator in words understood by humans. The challenge is real but not insurmountable. The above passage describes Jesus as the exact representation (Greek, *charakter*) of God's nature. The Greek term translated here as "nature" is *hupostatis*. The term *hupostasis* appears elsewhere in Hebrews as "substance" or "assurance": "Now faith is the assurance [*hupostasis*] of things hoped for, the conviction of things not seen" (Heb 11:1).

As such, God has a nature that is real, substantial, identifiable, and sure. He is not a mythical figure, as were the Greek and Roman gods. The English word typically rendered for *hupostatis* is "person." Such a word does should not automatically be equated in our minds with the many human beings we know. We have seen earlier that God is personal, relational, and has created humans in His image.

Based on the what the New Testament directly teaches, seven statements can be made about God.

1. There is one God.

2. The Father is God.

3. The Son is God.

4. The Holy Spirit is God.

5. The Father is Person.

6. The Son is Person.

7. The Holy Spirit is Person.

The result of the New Testament teaching, based on the words of Jesus and the writings of the Great Eight is that God exists eternally as Father, Son, and Holy Spirit. He is one God, a tri-unity. This tri-uness is expressed in the word Trinity. The term is not "Three." The meaning is three-in-one, a plural unity, One Triune God. This is different than a leadership group of three persons, which is known as "triumvirate."

CONCLUSION

As someone who was born and raised Muslim, I struggled when Christians spoke or wrote about "God in Three Persons." I envisioned three people walking down the street. I could not understand or appreciate how this could depict God Almighty. After serious Bible study over a period of decades, I learned that my mental picture of three people walking down the street was erroneous. Such a picture was a picture of three.

Indeed, God is one. Muslims, Christians, and Jews have always agreed on this fundamental point. In the New Testament, God clearly represents Himself as a three-in-one Unity. Exegesis of the text—the teaching that proceeds from the text itself—offers no other option. Orthodox Christian teaching springs from the New Testament itself. Christians have not imposed a subjective meaning upon the New Testament.

In the case of the Holy Trinity, the Great Eight New Testament writers harmoniously present this orthodox Christian doctrine. As with the previous doctrinal studies, their corroboration is broad-based and multi-referenced. The doctrine is based neither upon one verse nor upon one writer. Such a scenario makes it unlikely that the doctrine of the Triune God was a late imposition, or a hijacked invention thrust upon Christians. Jesus sent His disciples out to baptize new believers in the singular name of the Father, Son, and Holy Spirit—the name of God. The evidence suggests they did exactly that.

Chapter 9

Belief in Salvation by Faith in Christ

Muslims emphasize submission. Christians emphasize salvation. Similarities and differences exist between these two terms and two emphases. A brief treatment of this terminology may be helpful to Muslim scholars and thinkers at the outset of this chapter.

Both Christianity and Islam feature an unwavering belief in the afterlife. Both religions state that a person lives once and dies once. After this lifetime is over, each soul will face the Day of Judgment, or *al-Yom ad-Din*. The Bible and the Qur'an place great importance on the preparation of believers for that final day. Therefore, both Christians and Muslims are familiar with the same questions: What will happen to me on the Day of Judgment? What about the sins I have committed? How can they be forgiven? For Muslims, the prescribed preparation of *al-Yom ad-Din* is submission to Allah and his prophet, walking on *as-Sirat al-Mustaqeem*, the Straight Path.

Islam prescribes a combination of faith and works to bring the believer into submission to the will of Allah: Surah Ma'ida emphasizes the importance of both faith (*al-Iman*) and works (*al-'Amal*): "Allah has promised those who *believe and do good* His forgiveness and a great reward" (Q5:9, emphasis added). The Arabic words for believing, *amanu*, and working, *'amal*, are used in the verse. The Qur'an states that one's eternal destiny will be influenced by one's good works or bad works. "So as for those whose scale is heavy with good deeds, they will be in a life of bliss. And as for those whose scale is light, their home will be the abyss" (Q101:6–9).

THE BIBLICAL DOCTRINE OF SALVATION BY FAITH

Christians hold a different view of how believers come into right standing with the Almighty. As Christians often say, "faith is the *root* of salvation, while good works are the *fruit* of salvation." In other words, Christians are expected to accomplish good deeds, but these works are not the cause of salvation.

The Great Eight Witnesses utilized the words and actions of Jesus to form the New Testament doctrine of salvation. They assessed this to be the will of Christ on the topic. The brief summary of the Christian doctrine of salvation is this: Human beings are sinful by nature and action. They cannot save themselves. God, in His love, took on flesh, lived a sinless life that no other person ever lived, and then died on the cross as a sacrifice for sins. (This is based on the Old Testament model of substitutionary sacrifices, which will be discussed below.) Jesus not only died on the cross, but He rose again in the power of divine resurrection, signifying He had defeated sin and death. He offers this sacrificial exchange as a gift to all who would receive it by faith. Turning toward God and away from sin is known as "repentance" (Greek *metanoia*). Salvation results not only in forgiveness of sins, but also in spiritual rebirth and a new nature for the believer in Jesus.

For the Christian, salvation results from believing in what Jesus Christ, the Divine Savior, accomplished on the cross. It is a gift of God, received by faith. The work was done by Christ not by the Christian. The Bible refers to God's unmerited favor as "grace" (Greek *charis*). Technically, "salvation by faith" is shorthand for "salvation by grace through faith in the work of Christ on the cross."

Muslims frequently invoke the mercy of Allah, *bismillah ar-Rahman, ar-Raheem*. A notable difference exists between mercy and grace. Mercy describes God refraining from giving people the punishment they deserve. Grace constitutes the inverse. God grants people that which they do not deserve. Christ's grace results in unmerited favor, forgiveness of sins, and salvation. The type of grace described in this chapter is not assured in Islam, even though Allah may be merciful.

As mentioned above, some branches of Christianity have different ways of working out and applying this doctrine of salvation by faith in Christ. The biblical, historical position is described several paragraphs above. Catholics emphasize memorializing the death of Christ through the Lord's Supper. Before He died Jesus ate a Passover with His disciples. He broke bread to represent His body which would be broken. He used wine to represent His blood that would be shed on the cross. All Christians celebrate the Lord's Supper, which is also called "Communion," or even "the Eucharist." Many Catholics partake of the Lord's supper daily, which they see as a means of receiving grace. Protestants view the Lord's Supper as a memorial celebration of what Christ has accomplished on the cross.

Both Catholic and Orthodox churches place a general emphasis on the importance of the church for salvation. The Patriarch of the Coptic Orthodox Church once told an Egyptian Protestant colleague of mine, "You Protestants emphasize Jesus as the Door to salvation, but we emphasize Him as the Way to salvation." Indeed, Jesus is both the Door by which believers enter God's grace, and the Way by which believers journey this life.

THE WRITINGS OF THE GREAT EIGHT REGARDING SALVATION BY FAITH

Each of the four Gospels chronicles Jesus' life up to and including His crucifixion and resurrection. In the Synoptic Gospels, Jesus rises from the dead in the final chapter of each book, while in John's Gospel, Jesus' resurrection takes place in the penultimate chapter. As stated above, Jesus' death on the cross lies at the heart of the message of salvation by faith. Therefore, the majority of content in the four Gospels narrates events *prior to* the actual event of the cross. Nevertheless, the Gospels give ample evidence of the plan of salvation Jesus intended to bring about.

Matthew: The first Gospel presents unique material regarding the impending birth of Christ. Matthew captures the doubts and concerns of Mary's fiancé Joseph (Yusuf) when he learned that that the Virgin Mary had become pregnant. He considered perhaps calling off the marriage. At this time an angel spoke to him:

> But when he had considered this, behold, an angel of the Lord appeared to him in a dream, saying, "Joseph, son of David, do not be afraid to take Mary as your wife; for the Child who has been conceived in her is of the Holy Spirit. 21 She will bear a Son; and you shall call His name Jesus, for He will save His people from their sins." (Matt 1:20–21)

Therefore, in the first chapter of the New Testament, Jesus is introduced as one who will save His people from their sins. Indeed, Jesus' Hebrew name, Y'shua, means "God is salvation."

Mark: All four Gospel writers record the Last Supper which Jesus ate with His disciples. This traditionally took place the day before Jesus was crucified. Mark records Jesus as saying as He passed the cup among His disciples: "This is the blood of My covenant which is poured out for many" (Mark 14:24). Matthew would describe Jesus saying, "This is My blood of the covenant, which is poured out for many for forgiveness of sins" (Matt 26:28). Jesus emphasized the power of His blood to forgive sins. This was Christ's doctrine, not a later invention by the apostles or others.

John: The fourth Gospel begins its narrative with John the Baptist, who served as a forerunner for Jesus Christ. John the Baptist identified Jesus in terms of the Old Testament sacrificial system for sins: "The next day he [John the Baptist] saw Jesus coming to him and said, 'Behold, the Lamb of God who takes away the sin of the world!'" (John 1:29). John affirms what the other Gospel writers and Jesus Himself said about Christ being the sin-bearer.

Muslim readers are familiar with *Eid al-Adha*, the "holiday of the sacrifice." The concept of sacrifice (Arabic *qurban*) and atonement (Arabic *kefaarah*) are not otherwise prominent terms in Islam. The Qur'an does not feature the Old Testament sacrificial system in which worshippers were commanded to sacrifice animals as offerings for sin and guilt. The third book of Moses, called Leviticus, describes those sacrifices, including the annual sacrifice of the Azazel, or "scapegoat," on the "Day of Atonement" (Hebrew *Yom Kippur*). Jewish worshippers, even at the time of Christ, were conditioned to believe in and rely upon sacrifices for sins. Muslim thinkers should read the entire Old Testament, for the New Testament builds upon its themes. This "typology" occurs in John 1:29.

John 3 captures the nighttime dialog between Jesus and the Jewish ruling priest Nicodemus. In this discussion, Jesus introduced the concept of being "born again" or "born from above" (vv. 3, 7). Toward the end of this discussion, Jesus gave the famous statement about God's gift and salvation by faith: "For God so loved the world, that He gave His only begotten Son, that whoever believes in Him shall not perish, but have eternal life" (John 3:16). Once again, the writer places emphasis upon what God has given and what God has done. God grants everlasting life and forgiveness of sins to those who believe.

Jesus makes an important condition for believing, as recorded by John. In using the eternal "I Am" language, Jesus indicates that one must believe in Him as the Divine Savior: "Therefore I said to you that you will die in your sins; for unless you believe that *I am He*, you will die in your sins" (John 8:24, emphasis added).

In John 14:6, during the Upper Room Discourse, Jesus tells His disciples, "I am the way, and the truth, and the life. No one comes to the Father but through Me." Muslims will note that He did not pray for guidance to the way, or *as-Sirat al-Mustaqeem*. He stated that He was the way.

I indicated at the outset of this project that I would attempt to present passages that appear to contradict the main Christian teaching. Muslim polemicists have done this over the ages, of course. My purpose in doing so is that Muslim scholars and thinkers can make informed opinions on what Jesus said and taught. One such possible contradictory passage occurs in John 5:25–29, in which Jesus says:

> Truly, truly, I say to you, a time is coming and even now has arrived, when the dead will hear the voice of the Son of God, and those who hear will live. 26 For just as the Father has life in Himself, so He gave to the Son also to have life in Himself; 27 and He gave Him authority to execute judgment, because He is the Son of Man. 28 Do not marvel at this; for an hour is coming, in which all who are in the tombs will hear His voice, 29 and will come forth; those who did the good deeds to a resurrection of life, those who committed the evil deeds to a resurrection of judgment.

Several points can be taken into consideration. First, Jesus is speaking about people who had died in prior generations, before the event of the cross. Second, the term "deeds," which appears twice in the passage above, is not found in the original Greek, but is provided as deemed necessary for an accurate translation into English since "good" and "bad" are adjectives in English, not nouns. Third, the beginning of the passage states that those who "hear the voice of the Son of God will live" (v. 25). Ostensibly, the hearing will include believing. In conclusion, Christian theology is developed from a comprehensive reading of Scripture, factoring in the weight of supporting evidence in Scripture and any apparent rivaling interpretations. The entire weight of Scripture supports the Christian doctrine of salvation by grace through faith in Christ.

John provides summary rationales for both his Gospel and first epistle. These clearly state the doctrine of salvation by faith: "Therefore many other signs Jesus also performed in the presence of the disciples, which are not written in this book; but these have been written so that you may believe that Jesus is the Christ, the Son of God; and that believing you may have life in His name" (John 20:30–31).

John reiterates this doctrine in 1 John 5:13: "These things I have written to you who believe in the name of the Son of God, so that you may know that you have eternal life." Based on content such as this, Christians have humbly accepted God's promise of eternal life to those who believe in what Jesus Christ the Son of God has accomplished. Though Muslims may initially think it presumptuous when Christians speak of "assurance of salvation," Christians are simply stating what the Bible declares.

The Revelation vision given to John comprises the final book of the Bible. Revelation speaks of what will take place in the future, including the final salvation of believers. Jesus gives John a vision of heaven which states that salvation is from the Lord and belongs to the Lord:

> After these things I looked, and behold, a great multitude which no one could count, from every nation and all the tribes, peoples, and languages, standing before the throne and before the Lamb, clothed in white robes, and palm branches were in their hands; and they cried out with a loud voice, saying, "Salvation belongs to our God who sits on the throne, and to the Lamb." (Rev 7:9–10)

From the first chapter of John's Gospel through to the final Revelation, salvation is connected to the Lamb of God, Jesus, who takes away sins.

Luke: In his Gospel, Luke describes a woman who anointed Jesus' feet with perfume as an act of worship. At the conclusion of this interaction, Jesus speaks to the woman: "And He said to her, "Your sins have been forgiven." And then those who were reclining at the table with Him began saying to themselves, "Who is this man who even forgives sins?" And He said to the woman, 'Your faith has saved you; go in peace'" (Luke 7:48–50). Thus, Jesus affirmed both salvation by faith and His divine prerogative to forgive sins. This narrative corroborates Jesus' prerogative to forgive sins as seen in the Healing of the Paralytic in Mark 2.

After Jesus rose from the dead, He walked along the Road to Emmaus with two disciples who did not initially recognize Him. (Jesus' visage was glorified after He rose from the dead.) These disciples were disconsolate because they knew only that Jesus had died. In speaking to them, Jesus stated: "So it is written, that the Christ would suffer and rise from the dead on the third day, and that repentance for forgiveness of sins would be proclaimed in His name to all the nations, beginning from Jerusalem" (Luke 24:46–47).

The first major public preaching event in the Christian era occurred on the Day of Pentecost, which is historically referred to as the birthday of the global church. Luke narrates how Peter exhorted his listeners: "Repent, and each of you be baptized in the name of Jesus Christ for the forgiveness of your sins; and you will receive the gift of the Holy Spirit" (Acts 2:38).

Later, to the Jewish religious leaders who were persecuting the early church, Peter declared regarding Christ: "There is salvation in no one else; for there is no other name under heaven that has been given among mankind by which we must be saved" (Acts 4:12). Thus, Peter stated that salvation was uniquely given by Christ.

In the next chapter of Acts, Peter was summoned before the Sanhedrin. Peter was confronted with a hostile environment. Nevertheless, Peter told them: "The God of our fathers raised up Jesus, whom you put to death by hanging Him on a cross. He is the one whom God exalted to His right hand as a Prince and a Savior, to grant repentance to Israel, and forgiveness of sins" (Acts 5:30–31). Once again, the elements of the orthodox Christian doctrine of salvation by faith emerge: Christ's cross, repentance of the believer, and forgiveness of sins.

Luke chronicles several of Paul's sermons in Acts of the Apostles. During the first missionary journey, Paul gave the following message to a Jewish audience at Pisidian Antioch. The complete passage is presented here for context:

> Brothers, sons of Abraham's family, and those among you who fear God, to us the message of this salvation has been sent. 27 For those who live in Jerusalem, and their rulers, recognizing neither Him nor the declarations of the prophets which are read every Sabbath, fulfilled these by condemning Him. 28 And though they found no grounds for putting Him to death, they asked

Pilate that He be executed. 29 When they had carried out everything that was written concerning Him, they took Him down from the cross and laid Him in a tomb. 30 But God raised Him from the dead; 31 and for many days He appeared to those who came up with Him from Galilee to Jerusalem, the very ones who are now His witnesses to the people. 32 And we preach to you the good news of the promise made to the fathers, 33 that God has fulfilled this promise to those of us who are the descendants by raising Jesus, as it is also written in the second Psalm: "You are My Son; today I have fathered You." 34 As for the fact that He raised Him from the dead, never again to return to decay, He has spoken in this way: "I will give you the holy and faithful mercies of David." 35 Therefore, He also says in another Psalm: "You will not allow Your Holy One to undergo decay." 36 For David, after he had served God's purpose in his own generation, fell asleep, and was buried among his fathers and underwent decay; 37 but He whom God raised did not undergo decay. 38 Therefore let it be known to you, brothers, that through Him forgiveness of sins is proclaimed to you, 39 and through Him everyone who believes is freed from all things, from which you could not be freed through the Law of Moses. (Acts 13:26–39)

Paul brings forth several important points. First, he states at the outset in verse 26 that this is a "message of salvation." Second, he utilizes extensive Old Testament references, including a connection to David. Third, Christ suffered, was crucified and then He rose from the dead. "Through Him forgiveness of sins is proclaimed to you" (v. 38). Fourth, "everyone who believes is freed from all things" (v. 39). That is, Christ grants spiritual freedom to the believers whom He has freed.

Luke includes additional preaching narratives in Acts. Muslim readers are encouraged to conduct a full study of Luke and Acts.

Paul: Paul begins the Epistle to the Romans by stating, "For I am not ashamed of the gospel, for it is the power of God for salvation to everyone who believes, to the Jew first and also to the

Greek" (Rom 1:16). He explains this salvation in the third chapter of the same book: "For all have sinned and fall short of the glory of God, being justified as a gift by His grace through the redemption which is in Christ Jesus" (Rom 3:23–24).

Paul states that justification from sins is a gift of grace through redemption—what Christ has purchased. In the next chapter, Paul notes that Abraham was justified by faith, even back in the Old Testament era:

> What then shall we say that Abraham, our forefather according to the flesh, has found? 2 For if Abraham was justified by works, he has something to boast about; but not before God. 3 For what does the Scripture say? "Abraham believed God, and it was credited to him as righteousness." (Rom 4:1–3)

In Rom 4:3 above, Paul quotes what Moses wrote about Abraham in Gen 15:6, that Abraham believed God and it was credited to him as righteousness. Thus, Paul exhibits continuity with not only the other New Testament writers, but with the Old Testament writers as well.

Paul renders another confirmation of salvation by faith: "If you confess with your mouth Jesus as Lord, and believe in your heart that God raised Him from the dead, you will be saved; 10 for with the heart a person believes, resulting in righteousness, and with the mouth he confesses, resulting in salvation" (Rom 10:9–10). To the Ephesian Church, Paul describes salvation in this manner: "For by grace you have been saved through faith; and this is not of yourselves, it is the gift of God; not a result of works, so that no one may boast" (Eph 2:8–9).

Paul's connection to the Corinthian church has been described above. He thoroughly explains to them the doctrine of salvation by grace through faith in Christ:

> Now I make known to you, brothers and sisters, the gospel which I preached to you, which you also received, in which you also stand, by which you also are saved, if you hold firmly to the word which I preached to you, unless you believed in vain. For I handed down to you as of first

> importance what I also received, that Christ died for our
> sins according to the Scriptures, and that He was buried,
> and that He was raised on the third day according to the
> Scriptures. (1 Cor 15:1–4)

This sample of Scriptures will allow Muslim readers to form a clear picture of Paul's theology of salvation (soteriology). For further study, all readers are invited to read the New Testament in its entirety.

James: James, the half-brother of Jesus, and the leader of the Jerusalem Church, is often cited by Muslims and others in contradiction to the doctrine of salvation by faith. Indeed, James' writes: "You see that a person is justified by works and not by faith alone. . . . For just as the body without the spirit is dead, so also faith without works is dead" (Jas 2:24, 26).

On its surface, James' position seems similar to the Islamic position, and contrary to the orthodox Christian position presented thus far. How can Christians justify this apparent contradiction?

First, James in the previous chapter stated his position that the salvation of souls comes from the implantation of the word of God, which is the gospel: "Therefore, ridding yourselves of all filthiness and all that remains of wickedness, in humility *receive the word implanted*, which is able to *save your souls*" (Jas 1:21, emphasis added). Here, James clearly states that salvation is received, not worked for. The "word implanted" is the gospel message which the unbeliever hears, receives, and believes. James does exhort his audience to rid themselves of wickedness, which is consistent with the historical orthodox Christian position of repenting, then believing.

Note that repentance constitutes a turning of mind and attitude. It is not itself a good work. When unbelievers came to John the Baptist, Yahya, before the event of the cross, they asked what they should do. John emphasized repentance. He noted that good deeds were consistent with a repentant mind and heart. Yahya told those crowds:

> Bear fruits in keeping with repentance, and do not begin
> to say to yourselves, "We have Abraham for our father,"

> for I say to you that from these stones God is able to raise up children to Abraham. . . . And the crowds were questioning him, saying, "Then what shall we do?" And he would answer and say to them, "The man who has two tunics is to share with him who has none; and he who has food is to do likewise." (Luke 3:8, 10–11)

This interlude regarding John the Baptist's ministry confirms that James' insistence on repentance was not unique or contradictory to other New Testament preaching.

Second, James, in 2:23, immediately prior to the section quoted above, also quotes Gen 15:6, that Abraham was justified by faith. He explains further that God tested Abraham's faith by requiring him to offer his son. Abraham's willingness to do a certain work provided evidence for the faith that existed. Therefore, we may conclude that good works are the fruit of salvation, not the root of it. They constitute the effect, not the cause. However, if a believer has no good deeds at all, this may give question as to whether saving faith indeed exists.

Peter: Peter preceded James in leading the Jerusalem Church. Historians would naturally expect continuity in their respective teachings regarding salvation. Peter, as one of Jesus' inner circle disciples, shares extensively in his first epistle regarding salvation:

> Blessed be the God and Father of our Lord Jesus Christ, who according to His great mercy has caused us to be born again to a living hope through the resurrection of Jesus Christ from the dead, 4 to obtain an inheritance which is imperishable, undefiled, and will not fade away, reserved in heaven for you, 5 who are protected by the power of God through faith for a salvation ready to be revealed in the last time. (1 Pet 1:3–5)

Peter continues in the same chapter: "Knowing that you were not redeemed with perishable things like silver or gold from your futile way of life inherited from your forefathers, but with precious blood, as of a lamb unblemished and spotless, the blood of Christ" (1 Pet 1:18–19). In this first chapter of his first epistle, Peter states that believers are "born again" (v. 3) "through faith" (v. 5), in the "precious blood of Christ" (v. 19), the result being salvation.

Peter furthers explains his position on salvation in Christ: "He Himself brought our sins in His body up on the cross, so that we might die to sin and live for righteousness; by His wounds you were healed" (1 Pet 2:24). This section concludes with one additional verse from Peter: "For Christ also suffered for sins once for all time, the just for the unjust, so that He might bring us to God, having been put to death in the flesh, but made alive in the spirit" (1 Pet 3:18).

Peter affirms what the Great Eight taught: God saves souls. Humans cannot save themselves.

CONCLUSION

Christians consider salvation by faith to be the beginning of a believer's walk with God, not the end. As a believer walks with God, he or she will be transformed internally. The Bible calls this process "sanctification." Those wanting to study this further can study the topics of sanctification and holiness in the New Testament; these topics are beyond our inquiry at this time.

The Great Eight New Testament writers wrote extensively about forgiveness of sins and the salvation of souls. In unison, they presented a Christo-centric salvation. Specifically, they note that human beings are sinners who fall short of the glory of a holy God. God, in His love, came to earth in the form of the Divine Savior, the Lord Jesus Christ, who died on the cross and rose again from the dead. He shed His blood on the cross for the sins of people. He offers that gift of salvation to all who believe in Him. By His heroic act, Jesus has restored people to relationship with a loving, personal God.

The apostolic leaders of the early church carried this message into Africa, Asia, and Europe. Acts of the Apostles chronicles not only their words, but their actions also. Within one generation, they traveled and preached throughout the known world of that time. Though the gospel message encountered obstacles, and some people fell away from the faith, no evidence exists for a substantial hijacking of the core message of salvation by grace through faith in Christ.

The appeal made by Christians today seems relatively unchanged from that of the early church. God offers salvation in Christ. Any who will repent and believe do indeed receive salvation by faith in what Christ has accomplished. As the apostle John states, "We love, because He first loved us" (1 John 4:19). That is, God initiated salvation. All who live today enjoy the opportunity to be the glad recipients of that salvation.

PART IV

Outstanding Challenges

Chapter 10

Where Christians Have Gone Astray

THIS STUDY HAS EXAMINED data which indicate that the core teachings of Christian orthodoxy were faithfully transmitted by the Lord Jesus Christ, to the apostles and the early church. The Great Eight New Testament writers penned the twenty-seven books which comprise the New Testament to the life of Jesus Christ. These documents were canonized by early church leaders several centuries later, though they had been in circulation since the first generation of Christians. In broad chronological terms, the New Testament canon was officially adopted halfway between the writing of those documents and the advent of Islam in AD 610.

Previous chapters have chronicled the doctrinal challenges posed to Orthodox Christianity by heresies, including Ebionism, Gnosticism, Docetism, and Arianism. Muslims themselves have responded to doctrinal challenges to Islamic orthodoxy, such as those by the Baha'i and Ahmadiyya movements, just to name a few. In this regard, both religions share a history of defending their core, orthodox beliefs from heretical challenges.

A close examination of Christian history indicates that in various times and seasons many Christians and various churches have gone astray from orthodox Christian teaching. The New Testament provides the anchor for Christian orthodoxy and the safe harbor to which repentant Christians may return. Scant evidence can be provided that the core body of Christ has irreversibly strayed from Christ's intended desire, will, or teachings.

Nevertheless, some Christians in various times and places have gone astray. This section will briefly examine where Christians have gone astray.

ALL HUMANS, INDIVIDUALLY, HAVE GONE ASTRAY

The inquiry at hand considers the trajectory of the major religions—Christianity and Islam. These religions have core teachings which are well established and have been well known for centuries. At the outset of any discussion regarding straying from God's perfect plan, or *as-Sirat al-Mustaqeem*, it should be noted that all human beings *individually* stray. Isaiah writes, "All of us like sheep have gone astray" (53:6). Paul likewise writes, "All have sinned and fall short of the glory of God" (Rom 3:23). Christians and Muslims humbly concede the need for God's mercy and guidance. Nevertheless, this research focuses not on individual straying, but on the core teachings of a religion, since this will determine whether Christians, collectively, have gone astray. In other words, are the doctrines of the Bible leading people astray?

POLITICS ENTERING THE CHURCH

The rise of Emperor Constantine ushered in a new era for Christianity. His Edict of Milan in 313 changed the environment for Christians from one of persecution to an era of tolerance. That positive occurrence was offset by the palpable entry of political influence into the church, particularly in Europe and Byzantium.

The intrusion of political actors into the church can be traced historically down to the Holy Roman Empire. On Christmas Day AD 800, Pope Leo III crowned Charles the Great (Charlemagne) as emperor. The launch of the Crusading Era in 1095 by Pope Urban

II at Clermont-Ferrand, France involved political maneuvering on his part. The Great Schism of AD 1054, in which the Orthodox and Catholic churches formally split, was likewise more due to "church politics" and the use of different liturgical languages, Greek and Latin, respectively, than to significant doctrinal differences. These historical events mark departures from how the early Christians saw their faith and mission. However, the late dates of these events make it unlikely that they could answer the question of when, where, and how Christians may have become *ad-Daalleen*, those who have gone astray.

IMPROPER ELEVATION OF TRADITION OVER SCRIPTURE

Islam and Christianity place great emphasis on tradition. In Islam, the Hadith literature are the traditional sayings of the prophet. The early Islamic history from AD 610 to 661 feature the prophet's life and those of the *Rashiduun* caliphs. Serious Muslims place great importance on this era, particularly upon the Sunna of the prophet.

The words of the first apostolic generation remain important since these believers had been taught by Jesus. Those traditional sayings and teachings of Jesus and the apostles which the Holy Spirit desired to be retained were canonized in the New Testament. Paul wrote to the Corinthians: "Now I praise you because you re-member me in everything and hold firmly to the traditions, just as I delivered them to you" (1 Cor 11:2).

In later generations, some Christians went astray by elevating the extrabiblical traditions of men even when they contradicted Scripture. This had been a problem with Intertestamental Judaism as well. Jesus rebuked the Pharisees and scribes:

> And He said to them, "Rightly did Isaiah prophesy of you
> hypocrites, as it is written:
> > 'This people honors Me with their lips,
> > But their heart is far away from Me.
> > 7 'But in vain do they worship Me,
> > Teaching as doctrines the precepts of men.'

> 8 Neglecting the commandment of God, you hold to the tradition of men." 9 He was also saying to them, "You are experts at setting aside the commandment of God in order to keep your tradition." (Mark 7:6–9)

By emphasizing church tradition over Scripture, the Roman Catholic Church strayed from a number of biblical doctrines. One example was the elevation of the Virgin Mary above her esteemed biblical status. Since Jesus, as the center of the faith, came under continual attack over the centuries, an impetus grew to insulate Him by likewise insulating His mother Mary.

The Roman Catholic adopted three doctrines by tradition that are either contradicted by the Bible or upon which the Bible is silent. The first was the immaculate conception of Mary—that she was saved from sin immediately after her conception, unlike other people. Second, the Roman Catholic Church established a doctrine of the perpetual virginity of Mary, though the Bible mentions brothers and sisters of Jesus in Matt 13:55–56. Third, the Roman Church promoted the idea of the assumption of Mary, that her body did not see decay. This improper elevation of Mary has been called Mariolatry, and may explain why the Qur'an mistakes Mary as being part of the Trinity (see Q5:116). Unfortunately, Mary also became a focus of intercession, though this did not develop until centuries after the time of Christ. Nevertheless, Catholics have never believed Mary to be a person of the Holy Trinity. They have always believed the One Triune God to be Father, Son, and Holy Spirit.

A protest movement grew against this practice of elevating church traditions to be equal to Scripture. That movement coalesced fully in the Protestant Reformation of 1517, led by Martin Luther. Indeed, in the trials and debates between Luther and the Catholic leaders, the latter frequently appealed to church tradition as authoritative. Luther responded that "Solo Scriptura" ("Only Scriptures") are preeminent.

WHAT IS THE CHURCH?

Throughout this book, the term "church" has been used. Muslims are familiar with the term "mosque," *masjid*, and *jami'a*. It would seem "church" is just the equivalent term. While that is partly true, some further explanation is required for Muslim readers.

Muslims use the term "mosque" to describe the local assembly of Islamic believers. However, they usually use *umma* to describe the global community of Muslims. Christians use the term "church" to describe the local assembly as well as the global community. Additionally, most people also use the term "church" to describe the physical building where Christian worship is held.

While speaking to Peter, Jesus prophesied: "I will build My church; and the gates of Hades[1] will not overpower it" (Matt 16:18). Jesus saw the body of believers, also known as the body of Christ, as a group that would overcome evil. Paul prayed that God would be glorified in the church: "to Him be the glory in the church and in Christ Jesus to all generations forever and ever. Amen" (Eph 3:21). All institutions comprised of humans are imperfect. Neither is the body of Christ perfect. Yet, the church provides a glorious spiritual home to all who call on the name of Christ. This includes people of any background, including those of Muslim background.

CONCLUSION

For the purposes of this inquiry, the strayings examined above were committed by a subset of the Christian population at specific times in history. The New Testament, as delivered by the Holy Spirit through the Great Eight, provided the basis for correction. Furthermore, the political or traditional straying considered above happened much later in Christian history. Most of it occurred long after the advent of Islam. Therefore, it is difficult to make the argument that the Christian church strayed from a message that Jesus

---

1. Hades is a Greek word signifying the domain of departed souls. Some English translations render this term as "hell."

might have preached regarding him being an Islamic messenger of *tawhid*. To the contrary, the evidence indicates that the global church faithfully stewarded the main doctrines of Christian orthodoxy. Thus, this inquiry turns a corner to its final analysis.

Chapter 11

Muslims and the Status of the Claim of Christians Straying

In this final chapter, I speak as a person who was born and raised Muslim to others from the same background. Brothers and sisters, we will need great courage to reach the end of *as-Sirat al-Mustaqeem*. Be patient with yourself, but also be brave. Now we will recap the status of our inquiry.

SUMMARY OF THE INQUIRY

Christians believe that the Lord Jesus came into the world as God in the flesh. His purpose was not only to teach and do miracles, but also to die on the cross for the sins of mankind. Islam clearly teaches that Jesus was neither Lord, God, nor Savior. Muslims explain the contradiction between Islam and Christianity by simply stating that Christians have gone astray.

Islam retains a theological urgency for Christians to have gone astray. For if the beliefs of Christians are true, then Islam would have been unnecessary as a religion. While the concept of Christians straying constitutes a necessity in Islam, little Islamic research exists as to when, where, or how Christians went astray. This research has probed deeply into this critical question.

Chapter 2 advanced three leading Islamic theories into when, where, and how Christians may have gone astray. These will be reconsidered now. First, based on Q4:156–58, Allah allegedly deceived the disciples of Christ by making it appear that Jesus died on the cross when this did not actually happen. This theory creates a number of ethical problems related to the nature of Allah. For example, if Allah was prone to act in this manner, how then could Muslims be sure Allah did not make the prophet of Islam appear to be Abu Sufyan, or vice versa? The Muslim scholar Mahmoud Ayoub states that Fakr ad-Din Razi (d. AD 1209) questioned this substitution theory, since it would undermine any presentation of legal evidence. Any criminal being sought could simply argue that his likeness was cast upon another who actually committed the crime. Further, this issue does not solve the central questions related to the divinity of Jesus or the Trinity.

Second, Muslims have alleged that Jesus claimed to be a mortal messenger of *tawhid*, but that Paul hijacked Christianity. Chapter 5 considered the relationship of Paul to other early church leaders, who publicly called him "beloved." The apostle John, writing last among the New Testament writers, could have issued a clarion warning about Paul, yet he did not do so. Chapters 6–9 (Part III) consider Paul's theological output. Paul's writings made up one-quarter of the New Testament. Paul indeed contributed some unique ideas such as the "mystery"[1] of the gentiles' inclusion into the body of Christ, and the concept of the "fruit of the Spirit."[2] The data considered in Part III indicate that Paul concurred with the other seven New Testament writers on all the main points considered.

Third, the Islamic doctrine of *tahrif* has been a subcurrent of this study. Part II chronicled the relational and theological bridges from Jesus to His disciples and then to the Early Church leaders who canonized the New Testament. The scriptural and

1. See Eph 3:9.
2. See Gal 5:22–23.

historical information available suggest that these relationships remained intact. If the Bible was corrupted, this inquiry did not uncover when, where, or how that could have occurred. In fact, the evidence points to the contrary—that the Bible has been faithfully maintained and transmitted. Of course, Muslim scholars and thinkers are invited to make their own reading and evaluation of the Bible.

Finally, Part III provided a New Testament study of four Christian doctrines which are un-Islamic:

A. Belief in a Loving, Personal God

B. The Divinity of Jesus

C. The Triune God

D. Salvation by Faith

The data from the Great Eight Witnesses who wrote the twenty-seven New Testament books indicate a broad-based support for these central New Testament doctrines. No doctrine rests on the support of a single writer. At least six New Testament writers provided direct support for each of these central tenets of orthodox Christianity. Muslims ought therefore to consider these four teachings closely.

Dear Muslim reader, in our prayers we have sought refuge from Satan who whispers into the hearts of mankind, *"al-ladhi yuwaswisu fi-sudoor an-naas"* (Q114:5). Perhaps Satan is hindering you from considering these truths, or from embracing them in your heart. Satan is the deceiver. He is both accuser and accursed. He will be banished for eternity as *ar-Rajeem*. Today is the day to stand against him.

Moving forward, chapter 10 chronicled where Christians have drifted into ugly "church politics," or an improper reliance on church tradition. In such cases, the New Testament provided the source of authority and the map for correction. Additionally, chapter 10 noted that all people are sinners, who, like sheep, have strayed. Jesus is that Good Shepherd who can rescue the lost sheep.

However, this inquiry uncovered no evidence that the main body of Christian believers strayed permanently. They did not become irretrievably lost. Indeed, orthodox Christians confronted the heresies they encountered, countering them with the words, teaching, and sacred sacrifice of the Lord Jesus Christ.

Therefore, the inquiry into when, where, and how Christians went astray remains unsolved. The question persists for Muslim scholars and thinkers. Since the Christian faith spread so fast at the time of the apostles, it would seem that any straying must have occurred very early, prior to the faith taking root in faraway lands. However, Muslim and scholars may provide additional thoughts and theories about this.

Indeed, this has not been an exhaustive study. I did not have space to include all the New Testament references I recorded on each of the key doctrines. Time did not allow for a complete treatment of church history, though the previous chapters provided the most important events related to this research project. Finally, I provided a mere sketch of Christian-Muslim interaction regarding theological divergence. My goal was not to write an encyclopedia on the subject, but to simply provide a fresh look at one critical topic for readers of Muslim background in our generation. Due to the importance of the question *to Muslims* of Christians going astray, I felt it was necessary to address it at this time. Others may carry the conversation forward.

FAMILY MATTERS

Our parents, grandparents, uncles, and aunts tell us family stories. We seek to remember them as best we can, and to learn from them as best we can. So it is in my family, so it is in yours.

My own father faced a big decision as a young man. He set his feet on the path to become a medical doctor. Yet, he was from a small town. To study medicine required studying at medical school in the capital city of the Middle Eastern country our family is from. Since our family lived in a small town, my grandfather was not enthusiastic about his son moving to the capital. My father said his own father discouraged him from doing so.

My father, though not the rebellious type, felt that he had no other choice but to move to the capital for university and medical studies. This made for some family tension, of course. My father was successful in his studies. He then went abroad for his medical training and began his medical career. While abroad he met and married my mother. Shortly thereafter, my brother and I were born.

When I was two years of age, my family moved back to the same Middle Eastern country my father had a left a decade earlier. My father knew the need for doctors there was great. We moved into an apartment in the capital city. It turns out that since that time, my grandfather and almost all the family members had migrated from our ancestral hometown to the capital!

I have thought about this in relation to my own spiritual journey, and perhaps it may apply to yours as well. We seek the approval of our parents and loved ones. As much as possible, we seek to heed their advice. Perhaps some of your own loved ones have warned you about following Jesus Christ. Maybe you have received threats warning you not to become a Christian.

However, we, as humans, are limited in our ability to look forward in time. Just as my own grandfather later moved to the place he told his son not to go, many Muslims are following Jesus even after warning others not to do so. We live in a snapshot of time, yet we cannot see the wider sweep of history. Many Muslims are coming to Christ Jesus in our lifetime. Others may sincerely warn you not to worship Jesus, or read the Bible, or become a Christian. However, later they may do so. Perhaps your courageous example will give them added strength to set out on that journey as well. I say farewell with a poem. May God bless you.

> *We have prayed a prayer*
> *We have dreamed a dream*
> *We have searched for*
> *Sirat al-Mustaqeem.*

PART IV

Our quest begins with history
And ends with a date in eternity
What ties together both of them?
The Baby born in Bethlehem.

Now we have come
to our journey's end
Until next time,
Good bye, my friend.

Bibliography

Accad, Martin. *Sacred Misinterpretation: Reaching Across the Christian-Muslim Divide*. Grand Rapids: Eerdmans, 2019.

Athanasius. *The Deposition of Arius*. In *Nicene and Post-Nicene Fathers, Second Series*, edited by Philip Schaff, 4:334–42. Grand Rapids: Christian Classics Ethereal, 1891. https://www.ccel.org/ccel/s/schaff/npnf204/cache/npnf204.pdf.

Ayoub, Mahmoud. *A Muslim View of Christianity: Essays on Dialog*. Maryknoll, NY: Orbis, 2007.

Bukhari, al-. "Virtues of the Qur'an, (3) The Collection of the Qur'an." https://sunnah.com/bukhari:4987.

Encyclopædia Britannica. "Arianism." https://www.britannica.com/topic/Arianism.

Hilali, Muhammad Taqi-ud-Din al-, and Muhammad Muhsin Khan. *Interpretation of the Meanings of the Noble Qur'an in the English Language*. Madinah, Saudi Arabia: King Faud Complex, 1984. https://www.holybooks.com/wp-content/uploads/2010/05/english-quranalhilali-khan.pdf.

Ibn Kathir. "Commentaries for 1.7, Al-Fatiha (The Opening)." https://quranx.com/tafsirs/1.7.

———. "Commentaries for 4.157, *al-Nisa* (The Women)." https://quranx.com/tafsirs/4.157.

Irenaeus. *Against Heresies*. Translated by Philip Schaff, Idaho: Roman Roads, 2015. https://files.romanroadsstatic.com/materials/romans/early-christianity/IrenaeusV1-0.pdf.

Jawziyyah, Ibn ul Qayyim al-. "O Christ-Worshippers!" https://www.call-to-monotheism.com/o_christ_worshippers___by_ibnul_qayyim_al_jawzia.

Keith, John. *Translation of First Clement*. In *The Anti-Nicene Fathers: Translations of the Fathers Down to 325 AD*, edited by Allan Menzies, 9:229–48. 5th ed. New York: Scribner's, 1906.

Khalidi, Tarif. *The Muslim Jesus: Sayings and Stories in Islamic Literature*. Cambridge, MA: Harvard University Press, 2003.

Muhammad, Bilal. "Muslim Perspectives on St. Paul." Berkeley Institute for Islamic Studies, March 10, 2020. https://bliis.org/research/saint-paul-islam/.

Musaʾad, Ishaq, and Kenneth Cragg. "Introduction to the English Translation of *Theology of Unity*." London: Allen & Unwin, 1966. Arabic original: *Risalat at-Tauhid (Theology of Unity)*, by Muhammad Abduh, 1895.

Patrick, John. "Origen's Commentary on Matthew—Introduction." In *The Anti-Nicene Fathers: Translations of the Fathers Down to 325 AD*, edited by Allan Menzies, ed., 9:411. 5th ed. New York: Scribner's, 1906.

Quranic Arabic Corpus—Quran Dictionary. "Dll." https://corpus.quran.com/qurandictionary.jsp?q=Dll.

———. "Hrf." https://corpus.quran.com/qurandictionary.jsp?q=Hrf.

Ragg, Lonsdale, and Laura Ragg, trans. and eds. *The Gospel of Barnabas: Edited and Translated from the Italian MS. in the Imperial Library at Vienna*. Oxford: Clarendon, 1907. https://islamicbulletin.org/en/ebooks/new_muslim/barnabas_complete.pdf.

Razi. *al-Tafsir al-Kabir (The Great Commentary)*. Standard ed. Cairo: al-Matbaʾa al-Bahiyya, 1938.

Simnowitz, Adam. "Son of God in the Old Testament." *Biblical Missiology*, June 9, 2020. https://biblicalmissiology.org/blog/2013/02/11/son-of-god-in-the-old-testament/.

Stevenson, James, ed. *A New Eusebius*. London: SPCK, 1971.

9 781666 771831